COVENANT THEOLOGY: *A Baptist Distinctive*

In addition to the title you hold in your hands, Solid Ground has also produced two other titles that address the doctrine of Covenant Theology from a Baptist perspective.

COVENANT THEOLOGY: *A Reformed and Baptistic Perspective on God's Covenants* by Greg Nichols

"Baptists who embrace their historic Calvinistic and Covenantal roots have long since needed a robust and comprehensive treatment of Covenant Theology that includes the nuanced interpretations of the biblical covenants that a baptistic hermeneutic requires. This treatment by Greg Nichols does just that and more. As a devotee of the Westminster tradition (including its chapter, 'On God's Covenant with Man'), I differ here and there; sometimes significantly so. But there is so much to applaud in this volume and Baptists will do well to read this volume carefully and with much gratitude. A splendid achievement. I, for one, will insist that my Presbyterian students read it."
- Derek W. H. Thomas

"There has been an urgent need for Reformed Baptist to produce a work on the covenants. I am so thankful that Greg Nichols has engaged this very weighty work. It is a very timely addition on a vitally important topic and adds much to a growing Reformed Baptist literary body." - **James R. White**

THE DISTINCTIVENESS OF BAPTIST COVENANT THEOLOGY: *A Comparison Between Seventeenth-Century Particular Baptist and Paedobaptist Federalism* by Pascal Denault

"This book is a welcome addition to the literature on an issue that has vexed many for too long. It is clear that the seventeenth-century Particular Baptists' formulation of covenant theology in the Second London Confession of Faith was a modified version of the one contained in the Westminster Confession of Faith. But why the different formulation? Denault's work goes *ad fontes* (to the sources) to find the answer." - **Richard C. Barcellos**

"Pascal Denault deserves many thanks for his labor in researching and describing the nuances of English covenant theology in the Seventeenth Century. He has uncovered significant factors contributing to the differences between Presbyterian and Particular Baptist thought and practice, describing theological categories in easily accessible terms." - **James M. Renihan**

Covenant Theology

A Baptist Distinctive

Edited by **Earl M. Blackburn**

SOLID GROUND CHRISTIAN BOOKS
BIRMINGHAM, ALABAMA USA

Solid Ground Christian Books
6749 Remington Circle
Pelham AL 35124
205-443-0311
mike.sgcb@gmail.com
www.solid-ground-books.com

COVENANT THEOLOGY
A Baptist Distinctive

Edited by Earl M. Blackburn

First printing January 2013

*SPECIAL THANKS to Caleb Blackburn for his cover design.

ISBN- 978-159925-326-8

CONTENTS

CONTRIBUTORS

Earl M. Blackburn is the pastor of Heritage Baptist in Shreveport, Louisiana. He is the author of *Jesus Loves the Church and So Should You* (SGCB – 2010) and *John Chrysostom* (Evangelical Press – 2012) and contributed to the book *Denominations or Associations* (Calvary Press – 2001). He lives with his wife, Debby, in Bossier City, Louisiana.

Walter J. Chantry retired from the pulpit of Grace Baptist Church in Carlisle, Pennsylvania, in 2002 after 39 years of fruitful, pastoral ministry. He is widely recognized as a leader among Baptists, and has championed the Reformed faith for many decades. His numerous published works include *Today's Gospel: Authentic or Synthetic?* and *Praises For The King Of Kings* (Banner of Truth Trust – 1970 & 1991). He lives with his wife, Joie, in Waukesha, Wisconsin.

Ken Fryer is on staff at Heritage Baptist Church in Shreveport, Louisiana. An accomplished fine arts musician, he and his wife, Ramona, live in Bossier City, Louisiana.

Fred A. Malone is the pastor of the 175+ year old First Baptist Church of Clinton, Louisiana. His is also the author of *The Baptism of Disciples Alone* (Founders Press – 2003). He and his wife, Debbie, live in the metropolitan area of Clinton, Louisiana.

Kenneth Puls serves on the pastoral staff of Grace Baptist Church, Cape Coral, Florida and is the Editorial Director of Founders Press and Director of the online Founders Study Center. He and his wife, Celeste, and family live in Cape Coral, Florida.

Justin Taylor is Vice President of Book Publishing at Crossway and the proprietor of the Between Two Worlds blog, hosted by the Gospel Coalition. He has edited numerous books and served as the managing editor for the award-winning ESV Study Bible. He and his wife currently live in the Chicago, Illinois area with their children.

EDITOR'S PREFACE

When untaught and unstudied minds hear the words Covenant Theology, the first expression that often comes out of the mouth is "You mean infant baptism, right?" Why is it that many evangelicals associate Covenant Theology with infant baptism? Are these equivalent terms? Could it be because in many ways the evangelical world is theologically poverty stricken? Could it be that what was taught in theologically insufficient seminaries for decades has filtered down to form theologically ill-informed churches? Is there a connection between a less-than-focused teaching on biblical foundations and the mixing of theological terms? What began this root of change? One source is the Modernist-Fundamentalist Controversy of the early 20th century, which caused a paradigm shift in Evangelicalism from being primarily a theology-centered faith to an experience-centered faith. This shift is pointedly illustrated for many Evangelicals (and Southern Baptists in particular) in the well-documented teachings of E.Y. Mullins, former President of The Southern Baptist Theological Seminary in Louisville, Kentucky (then and currently the world's largest seminary). The decades that followed his installation in 1899 were impacted by his legacy that led away from an exegetical and systematic theological faith to a personal-experience oriented religion. Heavily influenced by the Liberal European theologies of Friedrich Schleiermacher and Albrecht Ritschl, which is clearly evident in Mullins' *The Axioms of Religion*, Mullins shifted from the Christ-centered, evangelical Calvinism of J.P. Boyce to the Liberal man-centered pragmatism of William James of Harvard and the personalism of Bordon Parker Browne of Boston University. This shift left a black hole in evangelical theological training and education, especially among the Baptists. The effect filtered down to the churches and is still in play today. Subjective experience has become the *sine qua non* of evangelicalism, instead of objective biblical, theological truth.

The purpose of this book is to correct such faulty thinking and demonstrate from Scripture and Church History that Baptists, from their earliest days until recent decades, believed strongly in Covenant Theology and did so without embracing infant baptism. While it is hoped that perhaps scholars and eminent theologians will read and interact with its contents, the primary aim is that pastors and the average person "in the pew" will be instructed and come to understand the delights of a covenantal interpretation of the Holy Bible and, thus, affect the grassroots people around them.

All the chapters and appendices of this book originally were made known to the public either through lectures, magazine articles, booklets, or blogs. They have all been, to one degree or another, substantially revised and edited from their initial offerings. Thus, a previous hearer or reader might hardly recognize them in their present, more mature form.

Special thanks are due to several people. In particular, the ARBCA Publications Committee, who asked me to undertake this project. Also, my editorial assistant, Courtney Brown (neé Kried) has given yeoman's assistance in the midst of my many pastoral labors. Four dear friends, who are all seminary professors, theologians, and pastors (Drs. Richard Barcellos, Fred Malone, James Renihan, and Samuel Waldron), carefully read chapter one and made many valuable suggestions. Though they may not agree with some of the final conclusions, their insights are valued, as are their cherished friendships.

In the spirit of the Bereans (Acts 17:11), this book is offered as a call to return to the historic faith of apostolic Christianity and the Protestant Reformation, which Baptists have championed since their inception. The editor humbly asks the reader to studiously ponder each chapter to that encouraging end. Soli Deo gloria!

> Great Father of mercies, Thy goodness I own,
> And the covenant love of Thy crucified Son;
> All praise to the Spirit, whose whisper divine
> Seals mercy, and pardon, and righteousness mine.
> *-Gadsby's Hymns*, #11

Earl M. Blackburn
Bossier City, Louisiana
Reformation Day, 2012

FOREWORD

Our covenant Savior sits upon a throne at His Father's right hand receiving the praise of all heavenly creatures. The saints of the OT and NT gone before us gaze upon His face with awe and wonder and love, both redeemed from sin in their times by the same blood of the crucified Lamb, slain by His Father's timeless decree before the foundation of the world. Songs of praise and adoration fall upon His ears while He delights in the joy of bringing many sons to glory. He reigns over all things as the Father's regent of all creation, working all things on earth for the gathering and good of His given ones from the Father. He has known His own before the world began and his own came to know Him in their time through the Word and Spirit; or rather to be known by Him in His predestined time.

For His sheep yet on earth, no heart's sorrow passes the Good Shepherd's sight without empathy, sympathy, and help. No heart's desire goes unknown and well considered. No life's moment exists without His design to conform them to His glorious image. He is the Prophet who gave them Truth, the Priest who sacrificed Himself for them, and the King who still captures their willing love and submission for their good. He is the Covenant Himself, the Mediator of His covenant salvation for His own. He is faithful to His promises, kind in His gifts, patient with their infirmities, and merciful to their sins. Before the foundation of the world, He received them as fallen gifts from His Father of Grace and pledged to enter His creation on their behalf as the only Redeemer and Savior from their sins. Now, having accomplished His saving work, He reigns supreme as the Lord of all, bringing each given one to His bosom of grace, preparing a place for them where sin and death are eradicated by His grace and power; where love and kindness are their daily and eternal pleasure. And, where the final regeneration of all things commences in eternity, the Savior will gird Himself and serve His beloved bride at the Marriage Supper of the Lamb.

Who has words to describe the glory this Beloved Son receives from the Father and returns to the Father for the display of such grace to sinners? Who can adequately describe the honorable attributes of His character or the infinite magnitude of His love and holiness? Who can form the words which adequately give thanks for so great a salvation which He has accomplished and bestowed at His Father's covenant command? This is our covenant God: The Father who decrees His covenant grace, the Son who appears to accomplish its gift justly, and the Spirit who joyfully carries that covenant grace to woeful and fallen hearts to give them new life...eternal life...to the glory of His covenant grace!

This is the Covenant Theology of the Bible. It is not meant to be studied nor debated by sterile minds and cold hearts. It is the exciting truth of the Eternal Father giving to His Beloved Son a fallen people for His own to redeem by His incarnate blood and righteous life; it is the humbling truth that One so divine would gladly agree to His own suffering for such sinners; and it is the miraculous truth that the Holy Spirit would invade the rebels hearts' to free them from their enemy's grip and to resurrect their dead souls to embrace by faith alone the covenant Mediator of their covenant Father. Truly, the Covenant Theology of the Bible is a wonder of God's infinite grace which brings Him eternal glory from the lips of those covenant sons and daughters who eternally give thanks to His glorious name.

It is my hope that this exposition of God's covenant grace by Reformed Baptists will once again inflame the hearts of Baptists everywhere to embrace the wonder of God's Covenant Theology and to live joyfully and obediently under that covenant grace forever.

The Problem

Sadly, however, amidst the imperfect knowledge and hearts of theological scholars, the wonders of God's covenant grace are sometimes hidden from Christ's sheep. Complex arguments designed only for theological giraffes, contentious spirits of party debates, or simply erroneous teachings sometimes douse the flames of God's covenant love with crippling distractions. The simplicity and purity of devotion to Christ sometimes suffers because of covenant confusion.

For the past fifty years, the resurgence of Calvinistic soteriology (i.e., the "doctrines of grace," the Reformed Faith, or the Five Points of Calvinism) among Baptists has been marked by disturbing distractions regarding God's Covenant Theology, creating disunity and further divisions between us. Some embracing Calvinistic soteriology have also embraced paedobaptist Covenant Theology and left our ranks for the warmer waters of Calvinistic Presbyterianism. Others, reacting to paedobaptist Covenant Theology, have rejected historic Baptist Covenant Theology as well, claiming that one cannot be a Baptist and still hold to Covenant Theology. Thus, historic baptistic covenantal theology (represented in *The London Baptist Confession of Faith of 1689*, hereafter *LBC*) has suffered an uphill battle for Calvinistic Baptist unity and for a confessional basis for associational fellowship and cooperative missions.

Adding to the confusion about and/or rejection of Baptist Covenant Theology are the various errors of paedobaptism, paedocommunion, Theonomy, neonomianism, Dispensationalism, anti-sabbatarianism, patriarchy, and hyper-Calvinism. Such errors are answered effectively by our historic Baptist Covenant Theology. However, the exponential explosion of books, conferences, blogs, sermons, and self-appointed internet teachers in the last fifty years has often made the proponents of our historic Baptist Covenant Theology a small voice in the wilderness of biblical errors.

Is there any hope of a robust Reformed Baptist Covenant Theology to stem the tide of errors distracting and dividing our Reformed Baptist churches? I believe that there is. Our Baptist forefathers faced many of these errors before and prevailed with a consistent Covenant Theology which served to expand Reformed Baptist churches from the seventeenth to the nineteenth centuries. In the last fifty years of the twentieth century, we have seen the multiplication of such churches beyond the dreams of our older pastors and members. Christ has promised to build His church on earth with the promise that the gates of hell will not prevail against it. Of necessity, His means is the faithful preaching and teaching of the Word of God which builds His church in each generation. We thank God for the progress of Covenant Theology among many more Baptists today and have genuine hope that the truths

COVENANT THEOLOGY: A Baptist Distinctive

contained therein will win the day against many of the errors mentioned above. God's unchanging truth will ultimately prevail to God's glory.

The Solution

This book is one attempt by confessional Reformed Baptists to explain, defend, and propagate a robust Reformed Baptist Covenant Theology among Baptists today. Its chapters are composed of several individual lectures, a blog, and some booklets previously published by the Association of Reformed Baptist Churches in America (ARBCA). While not proposed as a complete apologetic for a Reformed Baptist Covenant Theology, it serves well as a *primer* for the major tenets which we hold dear. Our hope is to encourage our people to embrace the biblical truths about our covenant God while presenting to others the "things most surely believed among us."

Pastor Earl M. Blackburn has authored a very helpful overview of the basic tenets of historical Covenant Theology in his chapter entitled "Covenant Theology Simplified." Along the way, however, he points out the distinctiveness of our confessional Reformed Baptist perspective. This is an excellent survey of historical Covenant Theology while at the same time explaining the Reformed Baptist perspective on the unity and diversity of the biblical covenants, the uniqueness of the New Covenant, and the role of God's Moral Law in His Covenant Theology. This chapter is an excellent overview of Reformed Baptist Covenant Theology which is easy to read and edifying along the way.

I was asked by the editor to contribute a chapter on "Biblical Hermeneutics & Covenant Theology." Hermeneutics (the science of interpretation) is indispensable to a correct understanding of the Scriptures. If you do not interpret the Bible correctly, you will believe and behave erroneously. Peter, writing with apostolic authority, informs us that no prophesy or part of Scripture is of private (Gk. – *idias*, where we get our English word *idiotic*) interpretation (2 Peter 1:20). There are *not* many interpretations of the text or passages of Scripture; there is only one. This chapter is intended to help the reader to correctly interpret the Word of God as it is set in a framework of Covenant Theology.

Rev. Walter J. Chantry has authored several chapters worthy of close study. His style is to pack much truth into his concise statements. Pastor Chantry's discussion of the "The Covenants of Works and of Grace" sets forth a presentation and defense of the two historical covenants in classic Covenant Theology. In a day when both paedobaptists and Baptists question or deny the Covenant of Works, his is a worthy defense of classic Covenant Theology for both. In the light of recent Calvinist dispensationalists' claims that one must reject Covenant Theology in order to be a consistent Calvinist (John MacArthur), Pastor Chantry shows clearly that Covenant Theology is at the very heart of Calvinism. Further, he calls for the preaching of both covenants to sinners and saints in the historic "law and gospel" theology for salvation and sanctification. His defense of the Ten Commandments as the Moral Law of God, first written on Adam's heart and later re-written on the regenerate's heart is a needed corrective to Reformed preachers everywhere and the lawlessness that abounds in modern society. Along with this corrective is the further defense of "The Imputation of Christ's Righteousness and Covenant Theology" in justification by faith alone. The current denial of this biblical truth by some professed Calvinists today is splendidly corrected in the light of a consistent Covenant Theology. To rob sinners and saints of this premier biblical truth weakens their comfort in salvation, their joy in sanctification, and their service for Christ's kingdom. Classic Covenant Theology still stands as the need of Baptists and paedobaptists alike to correct many errors and to uphold the fullness of our covenant God's blessings in Christ.

Along with Pastor Chantry's argument for classic Covenant Theology stands one of the distinctives of Reformed Baptist Covenant Theology in "Baptism and Covenant Theology." Taking on the historic paedobaptist position with charity toward our paedobaptist brothers, he reveals the inconsistencies and detrimental consequences of infant baptism. At the heart of his argument is the uniqueness of the New Covenant within the unity of God's covenants and the implications of that uniqueness upon the composition of the local church as baptized professors (believers) alone. This is more than just a minor disagreement among covenantal brothers. It is a major doctrine which is upheld by a consistent Covenant Theology for Baptists which forms our ecclesiological distinctive for building churches of professing disciples alone.

Finally, there are three appendices. The *first*, written by Justin Taylor, deals with a most controversial question "Was There a Covenant of Works?" It is the Reformed Baptist belief that a denial of the Covenant of Works undermines the gospel because this denial weakens not only the transference of Adam's sin, condemnation, and guilt, but the transference of Christ's righteousness, forgiveness, and peace as Paul lays out in Romans 5:12-21. The *second*, written by Ken Fryer, broadly sketches the belief of "Covenant Theology in Baptist Life." What is so contradictory is that most modern Baptists reject Covenant Theology that was the foundation upon which our denomination was built and grew strong. What was it that made Baptists the largest Protestant denomination in North America? What was it that made Baptists the strongest Protestant missionary force in the world? It was the foundational and Christocentric belief in Covenant Theology. The *third* is a simple comparison teaching chart written by Kenneth Puls entitled "The Old & New Testaments (How is the New Covenant not like that which has come before?)." These appendices are intended to clarify matters that have been alluded to throughout the book.

Summary

Every reformation and revival in church history has revealed ebb and flow in finding the stability of truth in the first generation for the growth of succeeding generations. In the New Testament, the first generation of Christians experienced competing arguments against apostolic truth in matters of justification, sanctification, and ecclesiology. Now we have the Apostolic faith once for all delivered to the saints to stabilize truth for each generation. However, the same debates resurfaced in the first generation of our beloved Reformation, requiring time and teaching to stabilize what we generally call "the Reformed faith." Once again, in the last fifty years of a resurging Reformed faith, we have seen old errors arising among paedobaptists and Calvinistic Baptists alike. History tells us that this is normal in every reformation and revival. We pray for a sifting out of old errors and an era of stability in this new day of consistent growth among Reformed Baptist churches.

Therefore, it is good to reiterate the "old paths" of a Reformed Baptist theology once held by our forefathers for a new day. A consistent Reformed Baptist theology will preserve church reformers and planters from the errors of paedobaptism, paedocommunion, theonomy, dispensationalism, neonomianism, antinomianism, patriarchy, worship wars, shallow evangelism, shallower sanctification, hyper-Calvinism, incipient Arminianism, semi-Pelagianism, and much more. Land mines are planted along the history of Covenant Theology which must be avoided by Reformed (covenantal) Baptists if we are to increase in unity and power for the growth of Christ's kingdom and church.

We Reformed Baptists love our Reformed and/or Calvinistic brethren and our non-Calvinistic brethren as we proclaim the unsearchable riches of God's grace in Jesus Christ our Lord. However, we must all follow our consciences informed by Holy Scripture as we labor in our corner of God's kingdom. Therefore, we pray that this little book will clarify our Reformed Baptist Covenant Theology and edify the pastors and saints building faithful local churches for the glory and honor of our covenant God. To our triune God alone be all the glory!

Fred A. Malone
Clinton, Louisiana
July 4, 2012

CHAPTER 1

Covenant Theology Simplified

Earl M. Blackburn

COVENANT THEOLOGY, SIMPLY STATED, is the view of God and redemption that interprets the Holy Scriptures by way of covenants. The Bible knows of only one Savior. In both the Old Testament (OT) and New Testament (NT), there is only one way of salvation: by grace alone, through faith alone, in Christ alone. The triune God is a covenant God who deals savingly with humanity through covenants. Both the Hebrew word *berîth* and the Greek word *diatheke* are used extensively throughout the Holy Bible and can be found in its most key and pivotal sections.[1] Though there is much discussion of the definition of a covenant, a divine covenant denotes a solemn arrangement divinely imposed, which places binding obligations upon the parties of the covenant. It is in this way that salvation is worked out in human history.

The Reformation brought a rediscovery of biblical doctrine and theology, not the least of which was a covenantal understanding of the Word of God. Reformed churches have long been distinguished for their adherence to Covenant Theology and, contrary to the thinking of most moderns, so have Baptists until the past eight decades. The Particular Baptists of the 17th century in England and the first Baptist churches in America made Covenant Theology a clear article of distinction in their Confessions of Faith and church constitutions, in

---

[1] The word *covenant* is used 301 times in its root and compound forms in the OT and 36 times in its root and compound forms in the NT, totaling 337 times.

which they set forth a magnificent view of the glorious grace of God.[2] Baptists of the 18th and 19th centuries continued in the same theological vein, as demonstrated so ably by the great Southern Baptist theologian and pastor, Dr. R.C.B. Howell:

> Salvation through Jesus Christ is according to 'the determinate counsel and foreknowledge of God' (Acts 2:23). He was pleased to make known to the fathers, His purposes in this behalf, in the form of *covenants*, which were of different characters, and revealed in various times. These covenants enter into the very nature, and pervade with their peculiar qualities, the whole system of divine grace. A perfect knowledge of the Gospel therefore, involves necessarily, a correct comprehension of the covenants.[3]

To their own detriment, many present-day Baptists have left their theological moorings. However, Reformed Baptists, following in the footsteps of their Baptist forefathers, have sought to return to those moorings and are covenantal in their theology. Reformed Baptists believe that to be consistently biblical (and Baptist) in interpreting Scripture (i.e., hermeneutics), one must be covenantal.

I. SOME PRELIMINARY CONSIDERATIONS & QUESTIONS REGARDING THEOLOGY IN GENERAL

A.W. Tozer's quintessential remark, which (reportedly) he repeated often, is worth repeating again, "We being what we are and all things else being what they are, the most important and profitable study any one of us can engage in is without question the study of theology." Theology is a delightful term that should not repulse anyone. It is simply the study of God and His truths and, of course, God's truths can *only* be found in His inerrant Word, the Holy Bible. Every true Christian loves God and His truths; thus, every Christian loves theology and, believe it or not, has a theology. Some may be able to articulate their theology better than others, but every believer has a theology. Because God's truth (theology) is only found in His inerrant

---

[2]*The London Baptist Confession of 1689*, Chapter 7, and *The Philadelphia Baptist Confession of Faith of 1742*, which is the "*1689*" with two additional chapters; see W.L. Lumpkin, *Baptist Confessions Of Faith* (Judson Press, Valley Forge, PA: 1959) pp. 348-353.
[3]*The Covenants* (Sprinkle Publications, Harrisburg, VA: 1994, reprint from 1855) p. 1.

Word, this does not mean that questions should not be asked in regard to the Word of God. In fact, good theology is often born out of asking good questions.

In light of the subject of this book, what preliminary questions should be asked? What about "Is there more than one Gospel?" The answer is a resounding "No!" From Genesis 3:15 forward, the only good news known to mankind is that of the promised coming One who will redeem sinners from sin and bruise the serpent's head. The only good news this world has ever known, from Adam to the end of time, is the great indicative of what God, in Christ, has done (see 2 Corinthians 4:3-7, 5:21).

Another question that may arise is "Does God have one or two ways of salvation, or is there more than one way of salvation?" Again, the answer is "No!" From Genesis 3:21 on, God saves people, not according to their works and what they deserve, but according to unmerited favor, pure and free. Salvation is not man's quest for God, but God's gracious quest for sinners. C.S. Lewis, the literary genius and Oxford don, laughed at the absurd notion of man's quest for God by likening it to the mouse's quest for the cat. Mice do not search for cats just as sinners, by nature, do not seek for God: Romans 3:11b declares, "There is none who seeks after God." Some teach that people in the OT, along with those in the millennium to come, were and will be saved by works (or some type of law-keeping or commandment-keeping).[4] There are two observations regarding this train of thought: 1) if people are saved by works, then no one would ever be saved. God is absolutely holy and perfect and the works of people, in order to be saved, would have to be absolutely holy and perfect. To think otherwise is to cheapen the entire biblical teaching of salvation; 2) if people are or can be saved by works or cooperation with God, then there was no need for a Savior or Deliverer to come into the world to save and rescue fallen, broken humanity.

---

[4] For example, Lewis Sperry Chafer, *Bibliotheca Sacra*, vol. 93 (Dallas Theological Seminary, Dallas, Texas, 1936) pp. 410, 421; also *The Scofield Reference Bible* and its many reference notes stating this belief.

"Does God have one or two or several purposes and a contingency plan should one fail?" Some teach that Christ came as Messiah to drive out the Romans from Jerusalem and set up an earthly kingdom from which He would rule and reign over the world. According to them, the Jews rejected God's plan and thwarted Christ's attempt to establish an earthly kingdom by crucifying Him. God's original plan failed; therefore, He turned to "Plan B" (the Church) and postponed the kingdom until the end of the age when there will be a 1,000 year reign of Christ upon the earth.[5] According to these, the Church is God's parenthetical afterthought and not His original purpose. Did God and the Anointed One fail in their original purpose, thus leading to a second purpose? The answer is an overwhelming "No!" God has always had *only* one plan ordered before the foundation of the world from which He has never swerved or been derailed, either by the Jews or any other people, and it shall never fail.

"Is there more than one people of God from Adam to the second coming of Christ?" Once more, the answer is "No!" Whereas the covenants of God have differed in their external administration, the underlying principle of "grace through faith" has always been the same. Every soul saved, from Adam to the last sinner converted before the second advent of Christ, becomes part of the one people of God. In heaven, the final abode of the redeemed, all God's elect shall be one. How is one brought into acceptance, right standing, and favor with God? It has always been by faith *alone*. Again, if one were saved by works or keeping the Law, then no one has been or ever will be saved. There is only One who has precisely kept the Law, who lived the flawless life, and died the required death that God's perfect holiness demands: Christ the eternal Son, the second person of the Godhead, the only begotten God. Abraham believed God, the Scriptures expressly declare, and it was accounted to him for righteousness (Genesis 15:6). All the OT saints, just like those in the New, were accepted and declared righteous before God by faith *alone*. Hebrews 11 boldly asserts the fact that the saints of the OT are at one with the saints of the NT.

---

[5] I was taught this as a young Christian, but these beliefs plagued me with many doubts and filled me with exegetical questions that the system could not answer.

"How is the Holy Bible to be interpreted—dispensationally, covenantally, or by forging a hybrid of both?" Historically, theologians over the centuries have interpreted Scripture covenantally. Though there have been nuances among the various covenant theologians, there remained the basic covenantal structure. The past 150 years has unveiled a new approach to interpreting Scripture called Dispensationalism, which is generally described in the above paragraphs.[6] Recently, some theologians, claiming new insight into the Scriptures and hoping to bring a degree of unity in biblical understanding, have endeavored to posit a hybrid between the two positions known as Progressive Dispensationalism.[7] They have created a new glossary of terms, in which they changed or by-passed the time-honored, orthodox vocabulary, in an attempt to fuse covenantal and dispensational frameworks. The synthesis that emerged leaves many questions unanswered, suffers from inconsistency, and neuters the Word of God of some of its most salient doctrines. It does not fit into a coherent, biblical interpretation. A mongrel will not and does not work, without the Scripture becoming humanly manipulated to say what someone desires it to say, instead of what God actually intended it to say.

"Is there not continuity and discontinuity between the Old and New Testaments?" It is obvious that certain OT practices no longer continue and there are particular NT institutions that are not found in the OT. However, there are also OT doctrines and practices that *do* continue and are carried over into the NT, forming an inseparable connection between the Old and New Testaments. Only when there is an objectively balanced, covenantal, and Christocentric interpretation of the Bible can it be rightly understood that salvation has always been by grace *alone*, through faith *alone*, in the Redeemer God *alone*, and giving all the glory to Him *alone*.

"Why has Covenant Theology been deemed the correct way of interpreting Holy Scripture?" The position elaborated in this chapter

---

[6] Clarence Larkin, C.I Scofield, John Walvoord, Dwight Pentecost, Charles Ryrie, et al.

[7] e.g., Robert Saucy, *The Case For Progressive Dispensationalism The Interface Between Dispensational & Non-Dispensational Theology* (Zondervan Publishing House, Grand Rapids, Michigan: 1993).

has been guided by a major academic principle brought over into biblical hermeneutics — *Ockham's Razor.* William of Ockham (England) sought to shave off or cut through the verbiage of complex arguments of the Scholastics and basically posited that the *simplest* answer is not only the best, but usually the *correct* answer. I agree wholeheartedly. Over the years, I have watched men strain, contort, and twist Scripture, draw inferences from non-biblical literature, and draw up complex and convoluted explanations that our Fathers would not recognize. In so doing, they have undermined the simple, proven orthodoxy of the centuries. This is to be cautiously avoided. Only when the entire Word of God is simply studied covenantally, properly balancing continuity and discontinuity, can one "rightly divide the word of truth" (2 Timothy 2:15).

Finally, something must be said concerning theological terms, phrases, and words. Allow me then to say a few words regarding *words.* From an exegetical study of the Bible (especially the NT), the early Christians were forced to do theology. They wrestled with the divine revelation of Holy Scripture, and saw that it was so "packed" that some biblical teachings could not be entirely or satisfactorily explained in a few words. An excellent example of the early Church doing theology is seen in the Christian classic *The Incarnation of the Word of God* (Latin —*De Incarnatione Verbi Dei*) written by Athanasius in AD 319. In it Athanasius, with exegetical precision, engaged the heretics who denied the Trinity and the deity of Christ, from both the Old and New Testaments, by utilizing a set of non-biblical words to help explain biblical truth. The Holy Bible, he realized, needed to be "unpacked," which sometimes required many words and a glossary of terms that enabled him (and other Church Fathers) to preach, teach, write, and discuss the gospel with clarity, simplicity, and understanding. Realizing the tension that still existed, which carried over from the 3rd century to his day, J. Gresham Machen confronted the modern and petty hostility to using non-biblical expressions:

> Many persons are horrified by the use of a theological term; they seem to have a notion that modern Christians must be addressed always in words of one syllable, and that in religion we must abandon the scientific precision of language which is found to be so useful in other spheres [e.g., medicine, science, technology,

economics, history, art, etc.] . . . I am perfectly ready, indeed, to agree that the Bible and the modern man ought to be brought together. But what is not always observed is that there are two ways of attaining that end. One way is to bring the Bible down to the level of the modern man; but the other way is to bring the modern man up to the level of the Bible. For my part, I am inclined to advocate the latter way. And I am by no means ready to relinquish the advantages of a precise terminology in summarizing Bible truth. In religion as well as in other spheres a precise terminology is mentally economical in the end; it repays amply the slight effort for the mastery of it.[8]

Facing accusation by the heretical Arians for using non-biblical terms to explain their beliefs about Jesus, the early church Fathers replied that God's truth is, at times, so compressed and rich that a plethora of human words and terms were needed to unfold and teach fully biblical truth.[9] Thus, human terms were constructed to teach and "unpack" biblical truths (e.g., *trinity, incarnation, virgin birth, deity,* etc.) No orthodox, conservative, Bible-believing Christian would deny these truths, much less the terms. In Covenant Theology, there exists the same concept of non-biblical terms used to explain biblical truths.

Opposition often arises today against those who use extra-biblical words to unpack and explain profound scriptural teachings. Admittedly, when a search is made of the entire Bible, terms like Covenant of Redemption, Covenant of Works, and Covenant of Grace cannot be found. It is a childish, simplistic attitude and a concordance, proof-text mentality that rejects these terms. It is often heard, "That word is not in the Bible" or "That's not a biblical word" or "Chapter and verse, Brother, or I will not believe it." Need the reader be reminded that the word *Bible* is not even found in the Holy Bible? Yet, this non-biblical word is utilized everyday by Christians and non-Christians alike. What

---

[8] *What Is Faith?* (Eerdmans, Grand Rapids, Michigan: 1925) p. 162-163.

[9] The sermons in the Book of Acts illustrate this assertion. What is understood is that all the preaching recorded in Acts is but a summary of what was actually said. A case in point is Paul's sermon on Mars Hill in Acts 17:22-31. Careful study of this sermon will reveal that Luke compressed into a few words what may have actually taken hours for Paul to declare. The same is true in theology. A concise theological term can convey what would take hours to explain or pages to write.

is the response to the accusation that pastors and biblical and systematic theologians use non-biblical terms to teach biblical truths?

As admitted above, there are terms used by covenant theologians that do not exist in the Bible. Lest anyone forget, a host of other words/terms *not* found in the Bible are employed by Christians everywhere to explain biblical truths. One classic example is the non-biblical term "Great Commission;" this expression obviously cannot be found in the Bible. However, when a Christian, who has but even the slightest knowledge of the Bible, hears this expression, his mind quickly thinks of Matthew 28:18-20. Many other non-biblical terms are used by Christians, pastors, and theologians every day, everywhere to convey scriptural truth (e.g., *canon, inerrancy, epistemology, hermeneutics, homiletics, monotheism/polytheism, theology, omnipotence, omnipresence, omniscience, aseity, incomprehensibility, providence, theodicy, Christology, passibility/impassibility, hypostatic union, peccability/impeccability, ascension, evolution, anthropology, Fall, soteriology, spiritual union, monergism/synergism, depravity, dichotomy, trichotomy, legalism, antinomianism, pneumatology, cessationism/continuationism, humanism/liberalism, annihilationism, excommunication, eschatology, rapture,* and *millennium,* to list a few[10]). These are all excellent non-biblical terms to help better communicate the truths or beliefs of God's Word to people, but they are absolutely *not* found in the Holy Scriptures.

Applying this identical concept to Covenant Theology is appropriately the same. The old adage applies that "if it looks like a duck, walks like a duck, quacks like a duck, eats like a duck, smells like a duck, and swims like a duck, then it must be a duck;" it is a duck no matter what it is called. The same is true for Covenant Theology. If it looks like a covenant, smells like a covenant, is treated like a covenant, acts like a covenant, and works like a covenant, then it must be a covenant, regardless of what it is called! A truth is a truth no matter what name is given to it. Strangely, some say they will *only* use biblical words when talking about certain theological positions, then use non-biblical terms

---

[10] Should the reader not be familiar with or understand some of these terms, a good dictionary of theology or systematic theology will help with the definitions.

when discussing or teaching other theological positions.[11] The various terms used in Covenant Theology, though not found in the Bible, express biblical truth and theological concepts. Could better terms be used? Perhaps. Nevertheless, exegetes and theologians through the millennia have found these terms user-friendly for unpacking all that God's Word teaches about covenants. Why then change or re-invent a theological vocabulary? Let us dispense with quibbling over human terms and arguing over expressions and instead, straightforwardly deal with what the Bible teaches and the concepts it sets forth.

II.   AN INTRODUCTION TO COVENANT THEOLOGY

While theologians and pastors have explained Covenant Theology in various ways, it can be reduced to three basic divisions: the first division is the Covenant of Redemption, which refers to the intratrinitarian agreement made before the world began in heaven among the members of the Godhead (the Father, the Son, and the Holy Spirit) to save elect sinners by grace alone. It is sometimes called the *everlasting* or *eternal* covenant or the covenant of *peace*. Although it is *not* mentioned *first* in Bible chronology, it is inferred and taught throughout the OT and NT as being foundational for all that takes place in redemptive history. The Covenant of Redemption is the chief and greatest of all God's covenants. The second division is the Covenant of Works, which teaches the universal sinfulness and guilt of humanity and the urgent need for redemption. It necessarily connects and segues into the next section. Finally, the third division is the Covenant of Grace, which is the revelation and outworking of the Covenant of Redemption on earth in time and history.[12] It, too, is based upon free grace alone and *flows* from the Covenant of Redemption. It is an overarching covenant, worked out in time through a series of subordinate covenants (administrations), starting with Adam (Genesis

---

[11] For example, some Calvinists state they will not use non-biblical, theological terms to describe their soteriological position lest they be misunderstood. On the other hand, they will employ the almost fifty non-biblical words listed above in discussing or teaching other theological positions. This is at the least inconsistent and at the worst duplicitous.

[12] The Latin terms for these three English terms are *pactum salutis*, *pactum ad opera*, and *pactum gratis*.

3:15, 21), finding its pinnacle with the New Covenant (Hebrews 8:7-13), and culminating in eternal glory in heaven.

Having given a brief introduction to Covenant Theology and its three main divisions, the next step is to examine each division more closely.

III.   THE COVENANT OF REDEMPTION

Just as there is no one single plot of land on the earth that yields every variety of flowering tree or fruit, so there is no one chapter of the Bible in which every truth of God is collectively revealed. God's truths are scattered throughout the sacred pages of Scripture and will not yield themselves to the slothful or lazy person who refuses to study. The exhortation of the writer of Hebrews applies here: "For though by this time you ought to be teachers, you need someone to teach you again the basic principles of the oracles of God. You need milk, not solid food, for everyone who lives on milk is unskilled in the word of righteousness, since he is a child. But solid food is for the mature, for those who have their powers of discernment trained by constant practice to distinguish good from evil" (Hebrews 5:12-14 - ESV). Therefore every believer (whether a theologian or student) must painstakingly study the entire Word, in its historical context, to grasp its correct intent and full meaning. Thus, one cannot carefully read the Holy Scriptures without coming across certain passages that raise the question of "What's going on here?" Several examples to illustrate my point could be given; however, two OT ones will suffice. The first example is Psalm 2:6-8:

> [6] "As for me, I have set my King on Zion, my holy hill." [7] I will tell of the decree: The LORD said to me, "You are my Son; today I have begotten you. [8] Ask of me, and I will make the nations your heritage, and the ends of the earth your possession.

Looking at this passage, several more questions arise. Who is speaking here? Who is speaking *of* whom? Who is speaking *to* whom? When did this conversation take place? What is being said? The answers are clear. David is the earthly person speaking. Writing under the inspiration of the Holy Spirit, he unveils a divine conversation between God the Father and God the Son that could have obviously *only* taken place in eternity past. In it the Father states that he will utter the decree. What decree? The decree the Father made with the Son to resurrect and *enthrone* the Son to status as the Redeemer and Mediator. Then the Father speaks and promises the Son a great heritage of souls from among the nations and the ends of the earth.

Another OT passage is Isaiah 42:5-7:

> 5 Thus says God, the LORD, who created the heavens and stretched them out, who spread out the earth and what comes from it, who gives breath to the people on it and spirit to those who walk in it: 6 "I am the LORD; I have called you in righteousness; I will take you by the hand and keep you; I will give you as a covenant for the people, a light for the nations, 7 to open the eyes that are blind, to bring out the prisoners from the dungeon, from the prison those who sit in darkness.

God the LORD introduces His special "servant" to Isaiah (and us) in verse one. The promise is made to this "servant" that He will be upheld by God and He will be given as a "covenant" to the people. Again, although the "servant" is introduced to Isaiah, in the prophet's time period, this conversation with and promise to the LORD'S "servant" could have *only* taken place in the eternal counsels of eternity past and it all speaks of future redemption. And, of course, this special servant is none other than Christ (see Philippians 2:5-11). These two passages speak of nothing more than what David states in Psalm 25:14: "The secret [Heb. *counsel*] of the LORD is with them that fear Him, and He will show them His covenant."

What is to be made of explicit passages in the NT, especially the Gospels, where Jesus issues claims about "as many" (John 17:2) or "all that the Father has given Me" (John 6:37, 39, 10:29, 17:9, 24; et al)? When were they given to Christ? Paul gives the obvious answer "before the foundation of the world" (Ephesians 1:4). Jesus uttered, "For the Son of Man goes [forth] as it has been *determined*" (Luke 22:22 – *emphasis added*). When was it "determined" that Christ would go forth to the cross? A few verses later Jesus says to his apostles, "And I appoint unto you a kingdom, as my Father has appointed [13] one unto

---

[13] The verb is *diatithemai*, the root of the Greek noun for *covenant + unto me*.

Me" (Luke 22:29). Jesus would afterward say emphatically that He had finished ("accomplished" - ESV) the work that the Father gave Him to do (John 17:4). What was the work given Him? When was the work given to Him? When was the kingdom appointed or "covenanted" to Christ? How are these words understood, if they are not interpreted as having taken place and determined in the eternal Covenant of Redemption? The apostles give further enlightenment in other parts of the NT Scriptures.

In Ephesians 3:11, Paul unfolds the "eternal purpose which God purposed in Christ Jesus our Lord." Peter, with the same exact comprehension of God's eternal purpose, declares that believers were redeemed by the "precious blood of Christ . . . who was foreordained before the foundation of the world, but was manifest in these last times for you" (1 Peter 1:18-19). John follows in the same train of thought by perceiving the Redeemer as a Lamb "slain before the foundation of the world" (Revelation 13:8). It was not that the Savior was actually slain before the foundation of the world, but in the intent and decree of God, it was established that the Lamb would be slain in human history. Thus, Professor Donald Macleod can say, "And that is why His work can be summed up by Paul in these terms: He was 'obedient unto death' (Philippians 2:8). Obedient to what? To the covenant [of redemption] stipulation."[14]

Some modern Baptists and evangelicals have commonly objected to Covenant Theology in general, and to the Covenant of Redemption in particular; maintaining its basis and terms are found nowhere in Scripture. An excellent answer to that objection is given by A.W. Pink, a mid-20th century Baptist:

> [L]et it be pointed out that, as there is no one verse in the Bible which expressly affirms there are three divine persons in the Godhead, coeternal, coequal, coglorious; nevertheless, by carefully comparing Scripture with Scripture we know that such is the case. In like manner, there is no verse in the Bible which categorically states that the Father entered into a formal agreement with the Son: that on His executing a certain work, He should receive a certain

---

[14] *A Faith To Live By* (Christian Focus Publications; Ross-shire, Great Britain: 1998) p. 98.

reward. Nevertheless, a careful study of different passages obliges us to arrive at this conclusion. Holy Scripture does not yield up its treasures to the indolent; and as long as the individual preacher [or believer] is willing to let Dr. Scofield or Mr. Pink do his studying for him, he must not expect to make much progress in divine things. Ponder Proverbs 2:1-5![15]

The Covenant of Redemption is not just a term devised by ivory-tower theologians to erect and bolster a man-made system; but rather, it is a biblical teaching springing from a scriptural basis. The particulars of it are that God planned to save sinners by *grace* alone (1 Thessalonians 1:4) and that this plan was developed in the eternal counsel and decree of God before time began (e.g., Romans 8:28-30; Ephesians 1:4; 2 Thessalonians 2:13; 2 Timothy 1:9; 1 Peter 1:2).

Two primary parties were involved in this Covenant: (1) the Father speaks of work given to the Son (Psalm 2:7-9; Isaiah 42:6-7); (2) though the Holy Spirit is not excluded, Christ the Son executes the prominent role in the Covenant pact and its outworkings. Jesus speaks of promises made to Him before coming into the world and repeatedly refers to a commission which He received from the Father (John 5:30, 43, 6:37-40, 17:2-12). (NOTE: The Spirit acts on behalf of the Father and the Son in the powerful carrying out of the Covenant of Redemption).

Also, two requirements appear in this Covenant: (1) the Father required the Son to assume human nature with its present infirmities, though without sin (Psalm 40:8; Galatians 4:4; Hebrews 2:10-11, 14, 15, 4:15); (2) Christ was to place Himself under the Law to pay the penalty for sin by His death and merit/earn eternal life and justification for those whom the Father had chosen (John 10:11; Galatians 1:4, 4:4-5; Romans 4:25).

In this Covenant, the Father made several promises to the Son: (1) He would anoint and assist the Son with the Holy Spirit (Isaiah 11:1-3, 42:1-4, 49:8, 61:1; John 3:34; Acts 10:38); (2) He would support the Son in His work (Isaiah 42:6-7; Luke 22:43); (3) He would deliver the Son from the power of death and place Him at His right hand upon His throne of glory (Psalm 16:8-11; Philippians 2:9-11); and (4) The Father

---

[15]*The Divine Covenants* (Baker Book House: Grand Rapids, MI: 1975) p. 18.

would send the Holy Spirit to form and finish the work of building the Church (John 14:26, 15:26, 16:13-14; Ephesians 3:9-11).

Finally, there are two rewards the Father promised Christ the Son in this Covenant that assured His success: (1) He would draw and preserve the elect unto eternal glory (John 6:37, 39, 40, 44, 45); and (2) He would grant to Christ a numerous seed from every "tribe, language, people, and nation" gathered from the ends of the earth (Psalm 2:7, 22:27, 72:17, 110:1; Hebrews 12:1-3, 13:20, Revelation 5:9). What is seen, from the above mentioned passages, is that salvation is not an after-thought, but a carefully fashioned and well-planned blueprint of the triune God to save poor, undeserving sinners.

IV.   THE COVENANT OF WORKS

The first biblical appearance of God making or establishing a covenant occurred at creation as the Creator covenantally built a universe and an environment in which mankind could live. The LORD later refers to this covenant when he spoke to His prophet Jeremiah—"if you can break my covenant with the day and my covenant with the night, so that day and night will not come at their appointed time ..." (Jeremiah 33:20). That covenant in the creation of the universe (and man) contained three distinct ordinances, which reveal the Creator's original intent for all humanity: (1) Sabbath; (2) labor or work; and (3) marriage (Genesis 2:1-25). These ordinances were for mankind's good and would be perpetually binding on all future humanity.

Within that creation covenant, God made the first man and woman, Adam and Eve. They, being created in and bearing God's image, were placed in the Garden of God called Eden, *which was a temple,* and were given a charge to "tend and keep it."[16] Why was the garden a temple? Because Adam and Eve experienced the full and wonderful presence of their Creator God in an indescribable manner (Genesis 3:8a) and worshipped Him perfectly. Some mistakenly believe that Adam and Eve were created innocent. On the contrary, they were created after the spiritual image of Him who created them in righteousness, holiness, and knowledge (see Ephesians 4:24 and Colossians 3:10). They occupied a moral relationship of uprightness

---

[16] This is sometimes referred to as the Creation Covenant.

with their Creator God, enjoying unprecedented communion with Him, being cared for by the abundance of the LORD'S provision, benevolence, and goodness. God constituted Adam as the natural head of all humanity. He was put into *and* under a probationary Covenant of Works, in which God promised that obedience would be rewarded with blessing and eternal life, and disobedience would be punished with curse and eternal death (Genesis 2:7-17).[17]

The language and structure of this passage is undoubtedly covenantal though the word *covenant* is not found in the entire section. Some argue that since the word covenant is not found in Genesis 1-2, there was no covenant; Adam, they reason, was *not* under any type of covenant or covenantal structure of any form. Thus, these critics are ensnared by what Justin Taylor calls the "word-thing fallacy," in which ". . . the absence of a particular term does not entail the absence of a particular concept."[18]

The first Man (Adam) covenantally stood as not only the natural head but also the federal head and representative of humanity and all his posterity (Romans 5:12-21). Adam was given complete freedom by God the Creator to do whatever he pleased, with *only* one prohibition— Adam must not eat of the tree of the knowledge of good and evil. The tree of life was in the midst of the garden/temple as a covenantal sign to Adam of God's promise of life and blessing; and the tree of the knowledge of good and evil was present as a test of Adam's covenantal loyalty. Would Adam believe and humbly obey God and be blessed, or would he willfully disobey God, break covenant with Him, and be cursed? The sad but inerrant account is given in Genesis 3:1-7. Adam yielded to the lie of Satan and willfully disobeyed and flagrantly transgressed God's *one*, and only *one*, holy commandment: he ate of the tree of the knowledge of good and evil. This is what is known biblically, historically, and theologically as the Fall of man. Adam's righteous status and subsequent disobedience are what make the Fall all the more heinous. The results of this one act of disobedience were quite evident. His communion with God was lost, his mind and

---

[17] Wayne Grudem rightly argues for not only the biblical teaching, but also for using the theological term "the covenant of works" in his *Systematic Theology: An Introduction to Biblical Doctrine* (Zondervan, Grand Rapids: 1994 & 2000) pp. 516-518.

[18] See Appendix I.

understanding was darkened, his emotions were twisted, his will was distorted and warped, and he, along with all his posterity, was cast into a state of spiritual deadness (Ephesians 2:1) that would eventuate in physical death. He was fallen, naked, ashamed, cursed, condemned, spiritually dead, and under divine judgment (Genesis 3:8-20); a constituted and actual sinner. Hopeless and helpless were Adam and Eve to remedy their situation.

Is there any connection between Adam and people through the ages down to our present time? Absolutely! To deny the transference of Adam's sin and guilt to his progeny is to fly wickedly into the face of Paul's entire argument in Romans 5:12-21, especially the undergirding truth of imputation, and is an insidious ploy to dismantle the gospel. Plainly stated, a denial of this biblical teaching, especially imputation of original sin and guilt, is heresy. God bluntly asserts in His Word that His just sentence of condemnation was imposed and imputed on every person because of the specific sin and transgression of the one man Adam, even though a person has not committed Adam's particular sin (see Romans 5:12, 14). A lawyer once explained to me the legal point that the driver of a get-away car is just as guilty of armed robbery as the person who went into the bank and robbed it at gunpoint. And so it is with Adam's sin. It is sin and guilt by criminal and familial association even though none of Adam's children ate of the "apple" or sinned in similar fashion as their first father.[19] It is a legal (forensic) fact that the grounds for divine imputation of sin and guilt upon all humanity stems from Adam's one act of disobedience. Thus, a person is a sinner before the person ever commits the first act of sin. The belief that people are not sinners until they sin is the ancient heresy of Pelagianism. The truth is people sin because they are sinners; they were born in sin and inherited a sinful nature from Adam our first father, from whom it was directly imputed and received. This is an exegetically established truth, instead of philosophical reasoning imposed upon the Scriptures, which some have erroneously assayed to

---

[19] This passage is the greatest in all of Scripture demonstrating the connection between Adam and Christ. It teaches the imputation of Adam's sin to all fallen humanity and the imputation of Christ's righteousness to all believing humanity. To deny imputation is really to deny the gospel. Professor John Murray points out in his highly recommended book *The Imputation of Adam's Sin* (P&R Publishing Co.; Phillipsburg, New Jersey: 1959) the verb "have sinned" in Romans 5:12 is in the aorist tense and literally means "all sinned" **in Adam**; pp. 9-21, et al.

do by saying "A person is not a sinner until the person sins." One cannot truly believe the Holy Bible and believe otherwise!

This is what many theologians have failed to understand and through their teachings have, subtly and oftentimes unknowingly, undermined the great salvation of grace *alone*, through faith *alone*, in Christ *alone*, to the glory of God *alone*. Professor Macleod provides the following explanation:

> Some people have enormous trouble with this because they find the whole notion of a covenant of works distasteful. But it is clear beyond a doubt that the reason why man was expelled from the garden was his disobedience. There is nothing whatever inherently improper in a covenant of works. Our very salvation rests on the obedience of the Last Adam and that obedience was in compliance with a covenant of works. Christ saved us by finishing the work given to Him to do (John 17:4).[20]

In summary, Adam represented all humanity (just as a diplomat or ambassador today represents all the people of his particular nation) and miserably fell. The far-reaching result is that everyone who has ever lived or shall live is inescapably connected to and a part of the Covenant of Works. Hosea the prophet's word to ancient Israel applies to every person today—"But like Adam they transgressed the covenant; there they dealt faithlessly with Me" (Hosea 6:7). Adam's sin is our sin! And, every person born or shall be born, by virtue of his relationship to Adam, is a sinner, transgressor, and violator of this covenant of works. Thus, everyone is still under its covenant obligations and curse. However, there is one person who kept and obeyed the Covenant of Works precisely, and only one—Jesus the second or last Adam (Romans 5:12-21). He came into the world and was born under the Covenant of Works, lived a life of perfect, active obedience to God's holy Law to fulfill the covenant obligation, and passively submitted to suffering and humiliation throughout His entire life. Christ's passive obedience culminated in His death upon the cross to bear the sins and curse of that covenant for those who repent and believe in Him. The merit of His entire life and work satisfied all the righteous requirements of the Covenant of Works and obtains for those

---

[20] *A Faith To Live By*, p. 93.

who believe in Him escape from the curse of that covenant. Through faith alone, His righteousness is imputed or accounted as our righteousness. As the breaking of the Covenant of Works caused Adam and Eve to be driven out of the Garden, so it should drive us to Christ; the one who was covenantally loyal to God for us in contrast to the one whom covenantally betrayed us.[21]

V.   THE COVENANT OF GRACE

It is now essential to consider the particulars of the Covenant of Grace, which is nothing more than the historical unfolding of God's eternal and redemptive purpose in Christ Jesus within time and history. The standard Protestant and Reformed catechisms teach that a covenant denotes a compact or agreement between parties, the obligations of which are binding. To a degree, this is true, but there needs to be further clarification. The concept of a covenant being simply an agreement between God and man is woefully deficient. A divine covenant is *not* an agreement between God and man that is mutual, bilateral, and conditional. As the noted 19th century (Southern) Baptist theologian J.L. Dagg correctly stated, "We are not to imagine, as included in this covenant transaction, a proposal of terms by one party, and a deliberation, followed with an acceptance or rejection of them, by the other parties."[22]   O. Palmer Robertson agrees: "No such thing as bargaining, bartering, or contracting characterizes the divine covenants of Scripture. The sovereign Lord of heaven and earth dictates the terms of His covenant[s]."[23] Instead, God's covenants, as manifested in the

---

[21] It must be carefully noted that even though Jesus Christ was born under the Covenant of Works and was a descendant of Adam with an Adamic nature (He was fully man), sin was *not* inherent to His human nature. He did not possess a fallen or sinful nature (i.e., bad heart or a bad record). Adam's sin is only imputed to Adam's earthly descendants. Christ (as the second Person of the Trinity) pre-existed Adam, and therefore Adam was not Christ's legal Head. The virgin birth ensured the union of a pre-existing person (God the Son) with a full human nature – thus the miracle of having Christ be *one* with the human race, and yet *not* one with Adam as His legal head. The imputation of Adam's sin to Christ was something that Christ voluntarily submitted Himself to on the cross per the stipulations of the Covenant of Redemption.

[22] J.L. Dagg: *Manual of Theology*; (Sprinkle Publications: Harrisburg, VA: 1982) p. 253.

[23] *The Christ of The Covenants*; (Presbyterian & Reformed Publishing Co.: Phillipsburg, NJ: 1980) p. 15.

COVENANT THEOLOGY: A Baptist Distinctive

Covenant of Grace, are administrations of His grace and *promise* sovereignly imposed.

Various passages reveal that some covenants, however, do have conditions attached to them. What about these conditions? While there are conditions attached to *some*, but not to all, of the covenants, they are not designed to destroy or annul the covenant. They are intended to bless those individuals who enter the covenant, as correctly asserted by Louis Berkof:

> God and man do not appear as equals in any of these covenants. All God's covenants are of the nature of sovereign dispositions imposed on man. God is absolutely sovereign in His dealings with man, and has the perfect right to lay down the conditions which the latter must meet, *in order to enjoy His favor* (*emphasis added*).[24]

It is absolutely imperative to understand that while there is just *one* Covenant of Grace, there are *different methods* of administering it; each being of gracious promise serving the *first* manifestation of the Covenant of Grace (Genesis 3:15), culminating in the New Covenant, and enjoyed in eternal glory. This is not a flattening of Scripture nor is it "a reductionism which has the tendency of fitting Scripture into our theological system rather than the other way around."[25] On the contrary, the one Covenant of Grace exponentially builds, increases, and heightens throughout redemptive history until it crescendos in heaven.

Furthermore, here is where even dissimilar theologians greatly err. For some, so vital is unity in their theological presuppositions regarding the Covenant of Grace that the diverse methods of administration are blindly overlooked or at least minimized. To other theologians, so vital is diversity to their presuppositions that the flow of redemption is sharply disrupted; connection among the various administrations is emaciated. Unity and diversity are not at odds with one another, but are equal and codependent upon each other. On the one hand, to stress diversity over unity fails to do justice to the whole plan of salvation, as

---

[24]*Systematic Theology*; (Wm. B. Eerdmans Publishing Co.: Grand Rapids, MI: 1941) p. 213.
[25]Stephen J. Wellum, "Baptism and the Relationship between the Covenants" in *Believer's Baptism: Sign of the New Covenant in Christ*; ed. Thomas R. Schreiner & Shawn D. Wright (B&H Publishing Group, Nashville: 2006) p. 127.

if God has two or three purposes or plans of salvation other than grace alone through faith alone, and torpedoes the eternal pattern of moral standards and righteous ethics. It makes our triune God changeable (i.e., mutable) and subject to defeat. On the other hand, to stress unity over diversity fails to do justice to progression in redemptive history and the progressive nature of God's revelation from the Old Testament to the New. It is almost as if some forgot that John the Baptist came baptizing and that he and the Savior inaugurated a *New* Covenant. Again, according to a remark by Dagg:

> Although God's purpose is *one*, we are obliged, according to our modes of conception, to view it, and speak of it, as consisting of various parts. So, the eternal covenant is one; but it is revealed to us in a manner adapted to our conceptions and to our spiritual benefit.[26]

Even though there is one Constitution of the United States of America, it has been administered differently during various stages of America's 250+ year history. In like manner, God's various methods of administration are called covenants, and are progressively revealed. It is extremely important to note that each covenant, and its administration, *is preliminary to the one that followed*, preparing for the final manifestation of the Covenant of Grace. What then are the subordinate, covenant administrations revealed in Scripture that make up the *one* Covenant of Grace?

THE EDENIC OR ADAMIC COVENANT[27]

After the Fall of Adam and Eve in the Garden of Eden, they ran from God and covered themselves with their own handmade garments.[28] God

---

[26]Dagg; p. 254.

[27] It is interesting to note that most of the moderns who classify themselves as of the school of Biblical Theology do not even deal with this covenant. e.g. Graeme Goldsworthy, *According to Plan: The Unfolding Revelation of God in the Bible* (InterVarsity Press, Downers Grove, Illinois: 1991), where he emphatically states that the "First Revelation of Redemption" in the Bible is seen in the Noahic Covenant (pp. 112-119). Genesis 3:15 is *only* treated incidentally and 3:21 is not even mentioned at all. J. Ligon Duncan has sadly noted that today "our divinity halls are mostly populated by 'biblical theologians', that is, merely thematic theologians with little time or capacity for synthesis" (found in a commendation of *A Faith to Live by*).

[28] Adam and Eve's actions are reflected in their children, the human race, today. "None seek after God" (Romans 3:11b); all run from Him and hope to make themselves look

sought out and came to them in unmerited favor and grace. Hiding from God, they heard the voice of God calling unto Adam "Where are you?" (Genesis 3:9). This is the *first* question ever asked in the Bible. It was not a question of ignorance, as if God did not know where they were, but it was a question of accountability. Their Creator who made them knew exactly where to find them, and our first parents (Adam and Eve) must now stand before Him and give an account for their disobedient and traitorous actions.

How terrible it must have been to hear the voice of God pronouncing judgment upon them. First the serpent is cursed. Then the woman hears the certainty of pain and punishment. And, last of all, the man who was entirely responsible for complete obedience is judged, found guilty, and placed under condemnation (Genesis 3:14-19). The episode of the Fall ends with the first man and woman being driven from the Garden of God to the east of Eden and losing the immediate presence of God. Their banishment proves they were under probation. Cherubim were stationed around the garden and "a flaming sword that turned every way" was strategically placed to keep Adam and his posterity from re-entering the Garden and eating of the tree of life.

In the midst of horrible judgment, grace is exhibited. Grace is displayed in two wonderfully strange ways: (1) at the end of cursing the serpent, a divine promise is made to send a bone-crushing Savior (in history/time, from the seed of the woman) who would bash the serpent's head and deliver men and women from sin and Satan's bondage (Genesis 3:15); (2) a sacrifice of an animal is unceremoniously reported. Mercifully in grace, God killed an innocent animal, made coats of its skin, stripped Adam and Eve of their handmade garments, and Himself clothed them with the tunics of skin from the slaughtered animal (Genesis 3:21). When most people read this Genesis narrative, they quickly gloss over verse 21 and give it little thought. Yet, it is of vast and foundational redemptive significance! Here, in the early days of the history of mankind, atonement and justification are typologically seen. Adam and Eve, though still under the curse of the Fall, are graciously forgiven, properly attired to stand in the presence of their holy Creator, and are

---

better by their own "fig-leaf" works of righteousness. The latent notion is to make themselves acceptable to whatever god they believe in by their good deeds.

taught the only acceptable way to approach God, especially in worship, is through sacrificial death and blood. This first administration in Eden is an *unconditional* covenant of promise and is prototypical of all of God's dealings in the Covenant of Grace. Again, it must be studiously noted, each covenant that follows is subservient to this first manifestation of *promise* and builds upon it.

THE NOAHIC COVENANT

Approximately 2,000 years later, the world had not gotten increasingly better, but worse. Adam's children wickedly followed in his footsteps so that it could then be said of them that the "thoughts of men were only evil continually" (Genesis 6:5). God the LORD was "grieved in His heart" and purposed to rectify the situation. He instructed Noah to build a uniquely designed water-going vessel, called an ark, to save his family and a select number and kind of earthly creatures. The LORD covenantally promised to spare Noah and all within the Ark. Then the rains fell for forty days and nights and the "fountains of the deep" were broken up. Eighteen feet above the highest mountains the waters rose and God destroyed the entire population of the earth with the Flood. Following the Great Deluge, God made a covenant with Noah (Genesis 6:18, 9:1-17).

Some would argue that since these verses contain the first mention of the word *covenant* in the Bible, there was no divinely-initiated covenant up to this point in redemptive history. What is shown here in God's interaction with Noah, they contend, is the beginning of a new covenantal structure in Scripture.[29] Is it the actual case that God is beginning a new covenantal arrangement? Or, in His mind, is God continuing a prior understanding of what He had already established? William Dumbrell takes exception to the claim that something novel was taking place and, elucidates that the joining of the two Hebrew words *heqim* (*to confirm*) and *berith* (*covenant*) depicts that "the institution of a [first] covenant is not being referred to but rather its perpetuation." And, as he later states, "that any theology of covenant

---

[29] See Paul R. Williamson: *Sealed with an Oath: Covenant in God's unfolding purpose* (INTERVARSITY PRESS, Downers Grove, Illinois; 2007).

must begin with Genesis 1:1."[30] Thus, the Noahic Covenant is a continuation of the *promised* fulfillment of the Covenant of Grace established in Genesis 3:15.

What is God's purpose in this covenant? Is He, after 2,000 years, deciding He will begin a new way of dealing with humanity via covenants? No. Instead, it is a unilateral covenant promise to Noah, who had just observed the almost indescribable destruction of all humanity. The unparalleled cataclysm he witnessed must have left Noah trembling and nervous with his mind filled with myriads of questions. What is the aftermath of God's destructive forces that lies before him in this soggy, water-saturated earth? What kind of world would he now encounter? Would it be inhabitable? Has the anger of God fully abated? Will the LORD do something like this again? Would it be morally irresponsible for Noah's descendants to conceive and bring children into such a world as lay before him? Will there ever be again summer and winter, seedtime and harvest?

To quiet his fears and assure confidence that the LORD would never again destroy the earth until all His eternal purposes had been accomplished, God inserts Himself into Noah's questions and *reaffirms* the creation covenant and institutes another covenant. It was made to all living, sentient creatures as well (Genesis 9:10), whether they trust in the triune God or not. This covenant unquestionably guaranteed "to maintain a stable world and keep mankind from destroying itself in order that the work of redemption might proceed."[31] Thus, there is no need to fear "global warming" and "nuclear winters" or "over population" and "deforestation" that is so prevalent in the news media. To eternally testify of His covenant faithfulness to keep His word, God placed a rainbow in the heavens as a sign. This magnificent sign, as Michael Lawrence observes, is "a symbol of God the warrior's bow, held at rest!"[32]

---

[30] *Creation and Covenant: A Theology of Old Testament Covenants*; (Wipf and Stock Publishers, Eugene, Oregon: 1984) pp. 26, 42.

[31] Keith A. Mathison: *Postmillennialism, An Eschatology of Hope*; (Presbyterian & Reformed Publishing Co.: Phillipsburg, NJ, 1999) p. 15.

[32] *Biblical Theology: In the Life of the Church*; (Crossway, Wheaton, Illinois: 2010) p. 59.

THE ABRAHAMIC COVENANT

The next manifestation of God's gracious Covenant was the one made with Abraham (Genesis 12-17). It, too, was a covenant of promise emanating from the previous ones. It is easy to focus on the particulars of this covenant, especially the sign of circumcision, and overlook the overall picture. Some have erroneously considered Abraham's to be "the" Covenant of Grace.[33] Exception must be taken to that naïve belief. Instead, Abraham's was just one more unfolding administration of the Covenant of Grace. God was moving forward to make good His promise of providing a Savior, which He promised to Adam in Eden. In His covenant with Abraham, the LORD further promised four things: (1) He would greatly multiply Abraham's descendants and give him numerous offspring; (2) He would give Abraham (and his seed) the land of Canaan; (3) He would be the God of Abraham's descendants; (4) He would bring forth a particular Seed, out of his general seed, through whom all the nations of the earth would be blessed. Who was this unique Seed? Paul the apostle tells us in Galatians 3:16 that this Seed was none other than Christ.

As a sign of this covenant, God required all males (only) *born* to Abraham, *bought* by him, and *under* his subjection, to be circumcised on the foreskin of their flesh on the eighth day (after birth). Note carefully that circumcision was to include also all male slaves and workers within Abraham's household and that it *excluded* all females. This sign was a mark of Abraham's "justification by faith previous to circumcision; therefore, circumcision could not be its cause."[34]

Circumcision distinguished Abraham's descendants from all the other peoples on the earth, as God was establishing a line through which the promised Messiah (i.e., the Seed) would come. Circumcision finds its

---

[33]A modern example of this is found in *Preaching Christ From The Old Testament* by Sidney Greidanus (Wm. B. Eerdmans Publishing Co., Grand Rapids, MI: 1999; p. 59) where the author not only makes the assertion that the Abrahamic Covenant is *the* Covenant of Grace, but also that it is the *first* establishment of the Covenant of Grace. This unstudied notion makes it seem as if God had done nothing during the first 2,000+ years of redemptive history to bring people into a saving relationship with Himself.
[34]Robert Haldane, *An Exposition of Romans* (Macdonald Publishing Co., Mac Dill AFB, Florida: 1958) p. 173.

fulfillment in the New Covenant, not in the outward sign of baptism, but in the inward seal of divine regeneration (i.e., circumcision of the heart) out of which flows justification (see Romans 2:28-29, 4:9-17; Philippians 3:3; Colossians 2:11).[35] Also contained in the Abrahamic Covenant was a promise of blessing to Abraham's children. Who, today, are the true children of Abraham? Jews, Arabs, those born of the flesh to believing Christian parents? Or those who are of faith? The Scriptures are very clear. It is *not* those born of the flesh, even if born to Christian parents (see John 1:13; esp. Romans 2:28-29), but only those who are born of God, whose hearts have been circumcised, and have saving faith in Christ Jesus the Lord (Galatians 3:7, 26, 29).

THE MOSAIC OR SINAITIC COVENANT

The next stage of the Covenant of Grace unfolds in God giving the Law (i.e., the Ten Commandments) through Moses at Mt. Sinai (Exodus 20:1-21; cf. Deuteronomy 5:1-21). This is often referred to as the Mosaic, or Sinaitic, Covenant. How are believers in the 21st century to view and understand the Law? Paul the Apostle instructs us that the Law is good (Romans 7:12) and gracious. Herein lies perhaps the most controversial aspect of Covenant Theology. Sadly, dear believers have fiercely divided over this issue. Nevertheless, the issue must not be avoided in hopes of maintaining unity. If a form of unity is held by refusing to study God's Law in redemptive history as revealed in Holy Scripture, it will be a false and fragile unity. It is not some, or much, or most of God's truth that is needed in this broken world, but all of God's truth. It is this author's contention that one of the reasons for such an anemic state existing in Christianity today is twofold: a deliberate perversion of (on the parts of some) and a gross neglect (on the parts of others) of the glorious gospel of Christ. However, closely aligned with this reality is a misguided understanding of the Law, which *indispensably* bolsters the gospel and, I might add, the Christian life. The Reformers, the Puritans, and the early Evangelicals rightly conceived and embraced the ancient formula of Law and Gospel.

---

[35]See Haldane: pp. 173-179. His entire argument and discussion on faith, justification, circumcision, and baptism in Romans 4:9-17 is exegetically cogent and very instructive. The exegesis of this Scottish Baptist theologian is an example of the biblical foundation of the Reformed Baptist position.

Even for those who did not possess it in printed form, the **work** of the Law has always been written on the hearts of all people since creation to either excuse or accuse the conscience (Romans 2:14-15).[36] As redemptive history progresses, the Law was given on Mt. Sinai in a visible, tangible shape and codified in tablets of stone. The Law was not *contrary to* or a *substitute for* grace, but a means of administering God's covenant more effectively to a redeemed community. A correct observation is given by Wellum:

> We must be careful that we do not equivocate on the term 'redemption.' In the OT context, it can simply refer to God's deliverance of the nation from Egypt without the full NT sense of redemption from sin and ultimate salvific blessings. To speak of the nation of Israel as a 'redeemed' people does not necessarily mean that they were all redeemed in the same sense that the church is the 'redeemed' people of God. No doubt there are typological relations, but the type is not the same as the antitype.[37]

As Paul notes in Romans 9:6b "that not all of Israel were of Israel," yet they were, generally speaking, a redeemed community. And, this redeemed community, who had been held long in pagan, Egyptian darkness, needed to be instructed in how to live before a thrice-holy God (Galatians 3:19-26). Professor John Murray emphasizes the grace element in the Sinai Covenant in its foundation upon the gracious promises to Abraham:

> We must not, therefore, suppress or discount these important considerations that the Mosaic covenant was made with Israel as the sequel to their deliverance from Egypt, *a deliverance wrought in pursuance to the gracious promises given by covenant to*

---

[36] When Paul states in v. 14 that the Gentiles did not have the Law, he did not mean that they had no knowledge of it. He simply meant that they did not possess it in a codified, written form as the Jews. He further explains that the Law's work was written, via Adam, on the Gentiles' hearts and had left its mark on them. Furthermore, this work and mark is seen when they do the things contained in the Law or their consciences' trouble them when they violate it, without possessing it in codified form. If the Gentiles did not possess the Law or the work of God's Law written on their hearts, how could their consciences accuse them? If not the Law, what moral standard would they possess by which to gage right and wrong, good and evil?

[37] Wellum, p. 134.

Abraham, wrought with the object of bringing to fulfillment the promise given to Abraham that his seed would inherit the land of Canaan, and a deliverance wrought in order to make Israel His own peculiar and adopted people.[38] *(emphasis added)*

What must be asked in regard to the Sinaitic Covenant is the following question:

> What was the nature and design of that covenant? Did God mock His fallen creatures by formally renewing the (Adamic) covenant of works, which they had already broken, under the curse of which all by nature lay, and which He knew they could not keep for a single hour? Such a question answers itself. Or did God do with Israel then as He does with His people now; first redeem, and then put under law as a rule of life, a standard of conduct?[39]

While there was covenant obedience demanded by God, the Mosaic Covenant was **neither** an absolute covenant of works for eternal life **nor** a historical renewal of that covenant made with Adam; already the Israelites were by nature under Adam's broken Covenant of Works and there was no need to renew it.[40] It was primarily a further fulfillment of God's gracious promises to Abraham for a people in the land of Canaan who gave generation to the promised Seed. Nevertheless, the

---

[38] *The Covenant of Grace*; (Presbyterian and Reformed Publishing Company, Phillipsburg, New Jersey: 1953) p. 21.

[39] Pink, *The Divine Covenants*, p. 142.

[40] Walter J. Chantry makes this observation, "When they talk about 'republication of the Covenant of Works' they confuse a number of issues. Of course the Covenant of works must be repeated in Moses and in the New Testament! In both we have the Ten Commandments insisted upon, which is how God established the order of this world (the Adamic Covenant). His holiness must shape blessings and cursings in his world in **all** ages! So we have a republication of the Ten Commandments in both Testaments. However, never after Adam is it suggested that men could have eternal blessings by keeping these commandments—but only by faith in the Seed of the woman who would come to destroy the works of the devil...Of course under Moses and the New Testament there are temporal blessings to be had by relative obedience to the Ten Commandments. Both under Moses and under Christ 'righteousness exalts a nation, but sin is a reproach to any people' temporally. Both under Moses and under Christ temporal family blessings result from keeping the commandments. So it follows that temporal blessings on earth come to businesses that follow Ten Commandment directions. But this is no return to a covenant of works! It is merely a demonstration of the rightness of God's laws for life in this world." (personal email, July 19, 2012)

COVENANT THEOLOGY: A Baptist Distinctive

conditional obedience to God's Law, required for the continued possession of the land, also was a proclamation of needed righteousness according to Adam's broken Covenant. Therefore, the giving of the Law as a covenant served to restrain their behavior, to condemn their sins, and to show their need of Abrahamic grace and faith typically revealed in the atoning sacrifices. Thus, the Sinaitic Covenant was added to the Abrahamic Covenant because of transgressions, yet still proclaiming the promised grace announced in Genesis 3:15 and confirmed to Abraham in his Savior Seed. In this manner, it was added as a subsidiary covenant to the Abrahamic Covenant of promise (both being a part of the Covenant of Grace) proclaiming Law and Gospel.[41] To believe that the Sinaitic Covenant is a republication of the Covenant of Works or an absolute type of covenant of works is to back-pedal in grace and create potential "dance partners" that are theologically dangerous.[42] Samuel Bolton lists nine arguments why the Sinaitic Covenant *cannot* be a covenant of works:

> (1) I cannot conceive that that could be called a covenant of works under which a holy God is married to a sinful people . . . described in Jeremiah 31-33;
>
> (2) That could never be said to be a covenant of works which had mercy in it to sinful men . . . as the apostle shows at length in Galatians, chapter 3;
>
> (3) If the law was given as a covenant of works, then it would be opposite to, and contrary to, the promise; but the apostle shows that this is not so: 'Is the law against the promises of God? God forbid' (Gal. 3:21);
>
> (4) That could never be a covenant of works which was added to the covenant of grace; but the apostle shows that the law was added to the promise (Gal. 3:19);
>
> (5) A fifth argument may be taken from Gal. 3:17: 'The law, which was four hundred and thirty years after (the promise), cannot disannul, that it should make the promise of none effect;'

---

[41] For a excellent discussion regarding the Sinaitic Covenant being part of the Covenant of Grace and *not* a covenant of works or a renewal of the covenant of works see Ernest F. Kevan, *The Grace of Law: A Study of Puritan Theology* (Baker Book House, Grand Rapids: 1965) pp. 113-126. Kevan demonstrates that this is the majority Puritan view and *is* the position of the *WCF* 7:1-6 (and, by implication, the *LBC 1689* 7:1-3).

[42] e.g.: New Perspective of Paul, Federal Vision, New Covenant Theology, and Dispensationalism.

(6) If it were God's purpose to give life and salvation to the lost sons of men by a covenant of grace, then He never set up the law as a covenant of works for that end;

(7) If the law were a covenant of works, then the Jews were under a different covenant from us, and so none were saved;

(8) God never appoints anything to an end to which the thing appointed is unserviceable and unsuitable [see Bolton's full explanation];

(9) It could never suit with God's heart to sinners to give a covenant of works after the fall; because man could do nothing; he was dead and powerless.[43]

Nevertheless, it was conditional in the form of works *only* in regard to possession of and external blessings in the land and in its reminder of needed repentance from sin. In this sense, it taught salvation by faith in the promises of the sacrifices and reiterated God's demand for obedience to His covenant while proclaiming salvation by grace through faith through the means of the sacrifices.

The Law in its three forms (moral, civil, and ceremonial)[44] was given for a purpose. It was to govern ancient Israel as a religious, spiritual nation and a typologically *redeemed* society (see Exodus 20:2), not a means of personal salvation, but as a way of living as a covenant people! This necessary distinction is carefully noted by one theologian who states, "Because sin was then so rampant in the world and Israel had acquired so many of the ways of the heathen during their long sojourn in Egypt, the Law was formally given at Sinai to serve as a restraint, and preserve a pure seed till the Messiah appeared."[45]

---

[43] *The true bounds of Christian freedom* (Banner of Truth Trust, Edinburgh: 1978) pp. 90-93. Editor's note: In all my varied reading on this complex and controversial subject, the simplest, most scripturally balanced and well-rounded exposition is that of Pink, *The Divine Covenants*, pp. 141-201. If you have not read it, read it. If you have read it, reread it.

[44] See Philip S. Ross, *From the Finger of God: The Biblical and Theological Basis for the Threefold Division of the Law*; (Christian Focus Publications Ltd., Ross-shire, Scotland: 2010). It is one of the most exegetical and scholarly works on the subject that has been published in decades. The bibliography alone is thirty-four pages, which demonstrates Ross' intense and irrefutable (in my opinion) interaction with contrary positions on many levels to exegetically prove that the three-fold structure of the Law is not of human devising, but of divine origin.

[45] Pink, p. 196.

Notwithstanding, Israel's history clearly records their failure to obey more often than their successes. Though individuals were saved by Abrahamic faith in God's promises, the nation broke God's covenant Law over and over. Yet, the LORD was not thwarted by their oft disobedience; He was true to His promise and preserved a seed through the nation from which sprang the Messiah.

The New Testament commentary on the giving of the Law also teaches us that it was given as a "schoolmaster" (i.e., tutor). How could it teach or tutor? By revealing sin in people's minds and hearts (like in ancient Israel) as Paul states in Romans 3:20b, ". . . for through the law comes the knowledge of sin." John affirms this same truth "Whoever commits sin also commits lawlessness, and sin is lawlessness" (1 John 3:4). Thus, by exposing and convicting people of their sins, it serves to bring unbelievers to Christ, that they might be justified by faith" (Galatians 3:24). The hymn writer exclaims it so wonderfully well:

> The law is good but since the Fall,
> Its holiness condemns us all;
> It dooms us for our sins to die
> And has no power to justify.
>
> To Jesus we for refuge flee,
> Who from the curse has set us free,
> And humbly worship at his throne,
> Saved by his grace through faith alone.
> -*Trinity Hymnal* (revised edition) #150

The civil and ceremonial laws were to pass away with the atonement of Christ, which will be examined later. But the Ten Commandments, which are the eternal, moral Law and a reflection of God's immutable and holy character, were never to pass away. As observed by Calvin Knox Cummings:

> The moral law [the Ten Commandments] has the same functions today as it did in the time of Moses. It is still God's means to convict men of their sin and to show them their need of a Savior. It still remains a standard of conduct after we have accepted Christ as our Savior. Christ delivers men from the curse of the law (Galatians

3:13), but not from the moral obligation to keep the law *as an expression of faith in and love for Christ (emphasis added)*.[46]

They are still binding as a standard of conduct for all peoples, in all ages, and especially to those who believe.[47]

Again, while the Mosaic Covenant was not a covenant of works for personal salvation, it did require from national Israel an obedience of heart and hands to the LORD, *if* they were to maintain their occupancy and tenancy of the land. If they turned from God their LORD, which they did on numerous occasions, they would lose the land. This explains not only the Assyrian and Babylonian captivities, but Israel's complete destruction in AD 70. They rejected God's Messiah, and God rejected them as His people.[48]

THE DAVIDIC COVENANT

As God's redemptive purposes continued to unfold, God made a covenant with David. It is sometimes called the royal covenant because it is made with Israel's quintessential king and speaks of his perpetual kingly lineage. Controversy has swirled around this covenant due to the fact that, as in the Covenant of Works and the Edenic Covenant, the Hebrew word for covenant (*berîth*) is nowhere to be found in God's interactions with David in 2 Samuel 7 and 1 Chronicles 17.

---

[46] *The Covenant Of Grace* (Great Commission Publications, Philadelphia, Pennsylvania: nd) p. 21. I acknowledge that his treatise has been most suggestive to me in several areas.

[47] While the Ten Commandments are perpetually binding on all peoples through all ages, there are certain attachments to some of them that have been abrogated in New Covenant days with the coming of Christ (e.g., one can now build a fire on the Sabbath and travel more than a Sabbath day's journey). Also, the threat and promise of the Second Commandment (Exodus 20:5-6) are rescinded because God no longer deals with children according to the obedience or disobedience of their fathers. (See a fuller explanation given below.)

[48] They broke the covenant (as it related to them as a nation) and did not enjoy His blessing. Thus, God divorced them and destroyed them as a nation. This is where there is another great confusion about the Mosaic Covenant. For the individual people of God (true believers) who lived under the Mosaic covenant, it was an administration of the covenant of grace. But for the nation as a whole, in terms of the *temporal* blessings promised, it was based on their covenant faithfulness. For differing views on whether the Sinaitic Covenant was of works or grace, see Malone (Chapter 2) and Chantry (Chapter 3).

Furthermore, the lack of a covenant ceremony, especially a sacrificial ratification, and a consequential curse further strengthen the antagonists' arguments. Once more Professor Murray dispels the senseless rhetoric of those who question:

> Although the word covenant does not occur in 2 Samuel 7:12-17, we must conclude that this is specifically the annunciation to David, which is elsewhere spoken of as the covenant made with David. In Psalm 89:3-4, the terms of 2 Samuel 7:12-17 are clearly reiterated. 'I have made a covenant with my chosen, I have sworn unto David my servant: thy seed will I establish forever, and build up thy throne to all generations.' And the same is true in later verses of the same Psalm (cf. vv. 26, 28, 34-37).[49]

What is this covenant God made with David? The immediate context enlightens us to its nature. The Ark of the Covenant, which represented God's immediate presence among His people, had been in exile since the days of Eli the priest (1 Samuel 4 ff.). David, after ascending to the throne of a united Israel, knew that his kingship could never be firmly established until the true King of Israel was properly brought from exile and rightly enthroned in Jerusalem over the entire nation. Thus, the first act of David as king was to fetch the Ark from the house of Obed-edom and usher it into his royal city. David's first act is of paramount significance. He humbly acknowledged that though he was the lawful king of a united Israel, he was not the supreme King; God the LORD was the supreme King of Israel. Immediately after David bowed to the rightful Sovereign, the LORD rewarded His servant. God entered into an unconditional covenant with him and promised there would always be one of his sons to sit on David's throne (2 Samuel 7:11-16, 23:5; cf. 1 Chronicles 17).

This covenant and promise is, of course, messianic. Why? Because many of the kings of David's line were ungodly men and, in the course of time, David's earthly line of kings ceased. Nevertheless, the covenantal promise continued and referred to Jesus the Christ, of the *seed* of David and great David's greater Son (Romans 1:1-4). Peter, the apostle, announced at Pentecost that this promise was fulfilled by the

---

[49] *The Covenant of Grace*; p. 23.

resurrection of Christ, whereby the Father raised Him from the dead and placed Him on David's throne (Acts 2:29-36). Peter's language does not refer to some future event thousands of years later, but is understood from the language of the NT that it took place with Christ's ascending into heaven and rightfully sitting down at the right hand of His Father as the mediatorial Lord of the universe. It is in that present position that Christ now, as David's son and David's Lord, exercises His three-fold ministry of Prophet, Priest, and King.

SUMMARY

All the covenants up to this point were not enough. God Himself, according to His own Word, found *fault* with the former administrations of the Covenant of Grace.[50] "For if that first covenant had been faultless, then no place would have been sought for a second" (Hebrews 8:7). Note carefully that the Old Covenant mentioned in Hebrews 8:7-13 is the Mosaic or Sinaitic Covenant of Exodus 20:1ff, which was all-inclusive of the former and preliminary covenants. Thus, being the paradigm and representative covenant, which incorporated *all* of the former covenants, the writer of Hebrews could deal with it in a prototypical manner showing that *all* the Old Covenant administrations were outmoded. Paul could speak with confidence as he referred to all the OT administrations as "the covenants of *the* promise" (Ephesians 2:12).[51]

The limitations and faults of the OT administrations are several: (1) the knowledge of the work of Christ was not clear and full; (2) the sacrifices had no power in themselves to save; (3) the Holy Spirit, though active and working, was not given in universal fullness; (4) the gift of salvation was confined almost entirely to the nation of Israel; and (5) people were saved in the Old Covenant, but not all in the Old Covenant were saved. Not everyone who was a legitimate and outwardly obedient member of the Old Covenant savingly knew God and was forgiven of his sins, or possessed an imputed righteousness.

---

[50]The fault found was *not* just with the weak and frail covenant members, but with the covenant *itself*. God Himself designed and made it faulty to prepare for a new and better covenant.

[51] τῶν διαθηκῶν τῆς ἐπαγγελίας. The promise, of course, being the one made to Adam in Genesis 3:15.

COVENANT THEOLOGY: A Baptist Distinctive

The Old Covenant had served its purpose. It had become obsolete, and there was a need for a new and better covenant.

VI.   THE NEW COVENANT

Jesus came to inaugurate the New[52] Covenant, which is the final stage of the Covenant of Grace. It did not come about unexpectedly, but was prophesied by Old Testament prophets. Ezekiel (36:25-27) speaks of the New Covenant period when God would take away the heart of stone and give a new heart of flesh (i.e., regeneration/new birth – John 3:3-8). Its most explicit prophecy is found in Jeremiah 31:31-34. Just before God promised His ancient prophet a New Covenant, He made a declaration of a change in administration of the Covenant of Grace (carefully read Jeremiah 31:29-30; cf., Ezekiel 18:1-32). The change has to do with God's manner of dealing with children. Notice exactly the wording of this proverb, one that was common in ancient Israel: "The fathers have eaten sour grapes, and the children's teeth are set on edge." In the past, this passage tells us, God dealt with children according to the status and actions of their fathers. If a father was a member of the covenant, so were the children. If a father was obedient or transgressed, the children also were blessed or suffered punishment accordingly (Exodus 20:5-6).[53] Jeremiah 31:29-30 (also Ezekiel 18:1-32) teaches that such would *not* be the manner of dealing with people in the New Covenant. As the prophet states in verse 30, "But each one shall die for his *own* iniquity; every man who eats the sour grapes, *his* teeth shall be set on edge." This instructs unmistakably that in the New Covenant each person will be dealt with individually, whether his

---

[52] "New" is καινην, from καινος, which is new in kind; as opposed to the other Greek synonym for new, νεος, which is new in time. This further enhances the point that the New Covenant is not the Old Covenant in new dress, but is a different type of covenant with a different method of administration.

[53] Several clear examples can be given to show that it was not a delusion that God visited the sins of the fathers upon innocent children: some of the sons of Korah (who sided with their father against Moses) and all the little children of Dathan and Abiram were killed even though they did not commit the same sin as their fathers (Numbers 16:26-32); so were the children of Achan (Joshua 7:24-25); Judah was put away because of the sins of King Manasseh (2 Kings 24:3, Jeremiah 15:4); Jeremiah complains that the people are bearing their fathers' sins (Jeremiah 5:7). These are not fallacious incidents, but horrible, bloodcurdling facts of Israel's history.

father is a believer or not, or whether his father has sinned or not. The standing of the father before God will have utterly no bearing on the place of the child in covenant dealings. The implications of this are far-reaching: a child would *not* automatically be included in the Covenant by birth or baptism, or simply because his father is a covenant member. By the same token, if a child is a member of a visible church in New Covenant days and his father is excommunicated, the child is not cast out along with the father.

Jesus, by His blood on the Cross, sealed the new covenant for His elect people. This is expounded in Hebrews 8:7-13 and 13:20. It must be precisely noted that there is a distinct difference between the Old and the New ("not according to the covenant that I made with their fathers" Hebrews 8:9a). The administration of the New would *not* be in the manner and practice of the Old. Here is biblical discontinuity.[54]

In the New Covenant, God irrevocably promises several things to each of its members that He did *not* promise to each member of the former administrations: (1) to lucidly and indelibly write His law on the mind and heart of each; (2) to be his God and make him part of God's people; (3) that every single one, from the greatest to the least, shall savingly *know* God. [NOTE: "Know" here is not a theoretical knowledge taught or catechized by a teacher, but is an experiential knowledge spiritually given.[55] Contrast this with 1 Corinthians 2:14.]; (4) that He would be merciful to all their unrighteousnesses; and (5) that their sins and lawless deeds He will remember no more. [NOTE: While these things were possessed by *some* members of the OT administrations of the Covenant of Grace, they were *not* possessed by every legitimate member **as they are in the New Covenant.**]

---

[54]This discontinuity is not dispensationalism, as some wrongly charge. Instead, it is an exact exegesis of the New Testament text, which seeks to handle Scripture faithfully without fearing or worrying about what opponents will accuse. Admittedly, there are tensions between continuity and discontinuity of the Old and New Covenants. Paedobaptists accentuate the continuity, while dispensationalists accentuate the discontinuity. The emphasis is not on one or the other, but on a careful appropriation of both, which Reformed Baptists, parrying thrusts from both positions, constantly strive to do.

[55]O. Palmer Robertson, *The Christ Of The Covenants*: pp. 293-297.

The New Covenant, being progressively revealed as the final administration of the one Covenant of Grace that supersedes and replaces all other administrations, is a more splendid covenant. It begs the question, "In what way is it new and how is it better?" It is new and better in the following ways:

One, there is a newness of administration. It is a fact that there is no more physical temple, Levitical priesthood, sacrifices, feast days, etc. *But* it is more than that. The newness of the New Covenant is seen in the way God deals with people. Again, it is extremely important to see and understand the difference between Jeremiah 31:29-30 (cf. Ezekiel 18:1-32) and Exodus 20:5. [NOTE: In this passage, there is a prophetic rescission of God's dealing with children *because of* or *through* their fathers. In other words, God rescinds His manner of dealing with not only the children of believers, but *all* children!] Each child will be dealt with entirely as an individual *instead* of having either the blessing or curse of his father upon his head.

Two, unlike the Old, the New Covenant ensures that the Law of God will be infallibly written on and put in the minds and hearts of not just some, but *all* of its covenant citizens. The *"work* of the Law" written" on the hearts of all people (Romans 2:15) since creation, is now made plain and uncluttered. When a person is born again (lit. "from above") and brought into the New Covenant, the laws of God are put into the minds and written indelibly upon the hearts. This putting of the laws in hearts and minds is not a metonym (i.e., an expression used as a substitute for something else with which it is closely associated) for regeneration, but is a special work that takes place within regeneration. The following verses bring this to light:

> **Romans 3:31** Do we then make void the law through faith? Certainly not! On the contrary, *we establish the law*. (*emphasis added*)

> **Romans 7:22** For I delight in the law of God according to the inward man.

COVENANT THEOLOGY: A Baptist Distinctive

Romans 8:1-4 ¹ *There is* therefore now no condemnation to those who are in Christ Jesus, who do not walk according to the flesh, but according to the Spirit. ² For the law of the Spirit of life in Christ Jesus has made me free from the law of sin and death. ³ For what the law could not do in that it was weak through the flesh, God *did* by sending His own Son in the likeness of sinful flesh, on account of sin: He condemned sin in the flesh, ⁴ that the *righteous requirement of the law might be fulfilled in us* who do not walk according to the flesh but according to the Spirit. (*emphasis added*)

Hebrews 8:10-13 ¹⁰ For this is the covenant that I will make with the house of Israel after those days, says the LORD: *I will put My laws in their mind and write them on their hearts*; and I will be their God, and they shall be My people.¹¹ None of them shall teach his neighbor, and none his brother, saying, 'Know the LORD,' for all shall know Me, from the least of them to the greatest of them. ¹² For I will be merciful to their unrighteousness, and their sins and their lawless deeds I will remember no more." ¹³ In that He says, 'A New Covenant,' He has made the first obsolete. Now what is becoming obsolete and growing old is ready to vanish away. (*emphasis added*)

Three, unlike the Old, the New Covenant cannot be broken. Under the old administrations, genuine members could stray and leave the Covenant, thus apostatizing, but not so in the New Covenant.[56] A

---

[56]Some have wrongly reasoned that just as Old Covenant members could leave the covenant and apostatize, so can members of the New Covenant. They ask, "Do not baptized church members turn back to the world and renounce Christ? It happened under Old Covenant administrations with those circumcised and it happens now." This thinking is erroneous in two ways. *First*, it equates membership in the visible church with membership in the covenant. They are *not* one and the same. One can be a member of the New Covenant and not be a member of the visible church. (Sad to say, this is seen in many today who have not understood biblical church membership.) Likewise, one can be a member of the visible church, obedient to its discipline, and still *not* be a member of the New Covenant. *Second*, it supposes that physical birth, (followed by baptism), brings one into membership of the covenant. This may follow logically, but it does not follow scripturally. Yes, baptized church members can and do renounce their confession of Christ and apostatize from the faith they once professed. However, this does not mean that they were once lawful members of the New Covenant and broke it, like circumcised, covenant-member Israelites did in the Old. Instead, their apostasy clearly shows they were never

false professor can turn and apostatize, but *not* a true covenant member. God prophesied to Jeremiah that, in the New Covenant, He would put His "fear in their hearts so that they will not depart from Me" (Jeremiah 32:40).[57]

Four, unlike the Old Covenant, *everyone* in the New Covenant, "from the least of them to the greatest of them," will savingly know the Lord forever. This is a fulfillment of what Christ said in John 17:2: ". . . as You have given Him authority over all flesh, that He should give eternal life to as many as You have given Him. And this is eternal life that they may know You, the only true God, and Jesus Christ whom you have sent." It more than just knows *about* the Lord, but the believer actually knows Him. When a sinner believes upon Christ as His Savior and Lord, that person genuinely and truly comes to actually know the living God. This does not exclude growing in grace and *knowledge* of the Lord, but one cannot grow in knowledge of a person until the person is personally known!

EXCURSUS ON THE LAW IN THE NEW COVENANT

The question must be asked, "What are the *'laws'* put into the minds and written on the hearts of new covenant believers (Hebrews 8:10)? Are they something 'new' or that which already existed?" The answer is quite simple—the New Covenant is *not* lawless or without law (antinomian). Christ proclaimed that He came to "fulfill" the Law and Prophets, not to abolish, abrogate, or destroy them (Matthew 5:17). The

---

legitimate members of the New Covenant. Their apostasy is proof: "They went out [from us] that they might be made manifest, that none of them were of us." (1 John 2:19).

[57]If a person is a member of the covenant today, he then is in the New Covenant. He is not in the Noahic, Abrahamic, Mosaic, or as some simplistically state "in the Covenant of Grace," but in the New Covenant. He then *partakes of* and *enjoys* all the blessings of the covenant as delineated in Hebrews 8:10-12. To say that one today, who is an actual member of the covenant, can truly turn away and lose covenant status is incipient Arminianism. Charles Hodge illustrates this error well when he says, "Do let the little ones have their names written in the Lamb's book of life even if they afterwards choose to erase them; being thus enrolled may be the means of their salvation." (*Systematic Theology*, vol. 3; Eerdmans Publishing Company: Grand Rapids, Michigan, 1982) p. 588. I am not saying that all who believe such are full Arminians, but it is Arminianism in its early stages. God says, in this verse that is impossible for a true believer to apostatize from Him in the New Covenant.

"laws" are nothing more than the eternal, moral, perpetual, abiding law of God as codified in the Ten Commandments. How do new covenant, gospel believers *"establish"* and *"fulfill the righteous requirements of the law"*? Is it not by keeping the entirety of the Ten Commandments (not just some *or* nine)? This is done out of love and devotion to Christ *alone*, (who saved us by grace *alone* through faith *alone*); these *alone* leads to gospel and joyful obedience?

Some theologians today will reluctantly admit that nine of the Ten Commandments are still in force, but the fourth commandment has been abrogated. For those who make such admission, questions must be asked. Why is it that 70 years ago almost every Protestant church, including and especially Baptists, believed in the perpetuity of the Ten Commandments? Furthermore, why was there absolutely no problem with Sunday, the Lord's Day, being the *Christian* Sabbath (as opposed to Saturday, the *Jewish* Sabbath)?[58] One of their arguments is that the Sabbath was *first* instituted in Exodus 16:23-30, later codified in Exodus 20:8-11, and was to and for Israel *only*. They ignore that in the codification of the Sabbath God references the Sabbath all the way back to creation—"For in six days the LORD made heaven and earth, the sea, and all that is in them and rested on the seventh day. Therefore the LORD blessed [not established] the Sabbath day and made it holy" (v. 11). The Sabbath is a creation ordinance established after the six days of creation and is to be perpetually observed through all ages unto eternity.[59] Heaven will be one eternal and glorious Sabbath. It was not

---

[58] Proof of the Judaeo-Christian ethic of Sunday being the Lord's Day or Christian Sabbath and churches holding to it as such, can be seen in the national so-call "blue laws." They prohibited government institutions operating, businesses being opened, sporting events being held, and numerous other things taking place on Sunday. The only institutions and organizations that were legally allowed to operate were law enforcement agencies, hospitals, pharmacies, and other emergency medical entities. In the late 1950s-early 1960s, States, yielding to secular pressures, slowly began to dismantle the "blue laws" of the Judaeo-Christian ethic. The destructive evidence of such dismantling is widely seen in today's secular society—Sunday is nothing more than a holiday of the world system and treated like any other ordinary day of the week, instead of a holy day of the triune God in which Christ's people are to assemble and celebrate the risen Christ and Lord.

[59] See Beale's detailed and brilliant discussion of the Lord's Day (Christian Sabbath) being a creation ordinance "The Church's New-Creational Transformation of Israel's Distinguishing Marks" in *A New Testament Biblical Theology* (Baker Academic, Grand Rapids, MI: 2011) pp. 775-801. See also Walter Chantry, *Call The Sabbath A Delight*

done away with by the New Covenant. Dumbrell astutely instructs in the following observation:

> It is noteworthy that when the Sabbath is legislated for (Exodus 20:8-11), it is brought not only into a framework of redemption, but also into particular connection with creation. . .For in pointing back to creation, the Sabbath points also to what is yet to be, to the final destiny to which all creation is moving.[60]

And, G.K. Beale (saying what Reformed Baptists have said all along) follows with this illuminating point:

> . . . the form of Sabbath celebration in this age on the first day of the week is the meeting of the church in worship. This weekly worship gathering commemorates Christ's inauguration of rest and points to the eschatological rest of saints gathered in worship of God and Christ through his word, songs of praise, prayer, and fellowship at the end of the age. Accordingly, saints in this age gather on the Sabbath to worship Christ and God by means of his word, praise, song, prayer, and fellowship, which foreshadow the greater worship of the new cosmos. This maintains the creational pattern of one day among seven that is 'blessed' and 'set apart' from the others (Gen. 2:2-3).[61]

Non-Sabbatarians argue that the church has come into **new** light and are no longer obligated to obey the Ten Commandments, especially the fourth. In particular, they argue that the Sabbath, not instituted until the time of the exodus (Exodus 16:23-26) and then only for Israel, has been abolished because it was a sign or shadow anticipating the salvation-rest already realized by the work of Christ (Matthew 11:28; Colossians 2:17; etc.). It is often heard, "I find my rest in Christ every day and do not need a special day." Oh really? Then why does the writer of Hebrews teach that there *is* (present tense), here and now, a rest-day

---

(The Banner Of Truth Trust, Edinburgh: 1991); Joseph A. Pipa, *The Lord's Day* (Christian Focus Publication, Ross-shire, Great Britain: 1997).
[60] *Creation and Covenant*; p. 35.
[61] Beale, p. 796-7.

festival (Gk. *sabbatismos*) for the people of God (Hebrews 4:9)? [62] Has the church indeed come into **new** light? Have we discovered **new** exegetical methods that have only been unearthed in the last half century? Have we become wiser with **new** truth than the Reformers, the Puritans, the great Evangelists of Jonathan Edwards' era, our Baptist forefathers, and the patriarchs of the modern missions movement? Has society improved with this **new** hermeneutic? With the Gallup Poll telling us that more people attend sporting events on Sunday than houses of worship and people allowing any sporting event or social and family occasion to cause them to forsake their assembling with the people of Christ in worship (see Hebrews 10:25) than ever before, has the Church grown stronger? Has the gospel gotten purer? Overall, has zeal and passion for Christ increased? Has the burden and flame to carry Christ and His holy gospel to the ends of the earth expanded? The obvious answer to all these questions is a resounding "No!" It was Mr. Spurgeon himself who said, "Whatever is true in theology is not **new**, and whatever is **new** is not true."

Richard B. Gaffin correctly answers the non-Sabbatarians with principled and exegetical arguments:

> 1. that the weekly Sabbath is a 'creation ordinance,' that is, based on the action of God in blessing, hallowing, and himself resting on the seventh day at creation, before the fall (Gen. 2:3; Ex. 20:11, 31:17); 2. that the Sabbath commandment, because it is included in the Decalogue (Ex. 20:8-11; Dt. 5:12-15), is part of God's enduring moral law; 3. that the writer of Hebrews teaches that the weekly Sabbath-sign [the Lord's Day] points to the eschatological rest-order, anticipated by God already at creation and secured, in view of the fall, by the redemptive work of Christ, but which will not be [fully] entered by the people of God until Christ's return (Heb. 4:3b-4, 9-11; 9:28).[63]

---

[62] See John Owen, *Hebrews*, vol. 2 "Concerning A Day Of Sacred Rest" (Banner of Truth Trust, Edinburgh: 1991) pp. 263-437. In my opinion no one has ever answered Owen's exegetical arguments.

[63] *New Dictionary of Theology*, ed. Sinclair B. Ferguson, David F. Wright, J.I. Packer (InterVarsity Press, Leicester, England: 1988) p. 606.

CONCLUSIVE SUPERIORITY OF THE NEW COVENANT

No better conclusion could be given than that which the apostle delineates and contrasts in 2 Corinthians 3:7-18. This passage teaches that the New Covenant is not waiting to be enacted, but is in force now. If the ministry of the letter was glorious, how much **more** is the ministry of the Spirit (v. 6)? If the ministry of death was glorious, how much **more** glorious is the ministry of the life (v. 7-8)? If the ministry of condemnation had glory, how much **more** does the ministry of righteousness (v. 9)? If the ministry of glory, comparatively speaking, had no glory, how much **more** the ministry that excels (v. 10)? If the ministry that passed away was glorious, how much **more** glorious is the ministry that remains (v. 11)? If the ministry that was veiled was glorious, how much **more** the ministry that is unveiled (v. 12-18)? The New Covenant is vastly superior to all that preceded it. Furthermore, these points demonstrate the beauty, glory, and superiority of the New Covenant, which *shall not* and *cannot* be personally annulled. The New Covenant will find its culmination when Christ returns and the glory of the world to come is ushered in.

VII.   THE PURPOSE OF THE COVENANT OF GRACE

It is important to remember that the several administrations of the subordinate covenants, in the *one* Covenant of Grace, serve a twofold purpose. The *first* purpose is to increase redemptive light and to reveal the knowledge of the glory of God in the face of Jesus Christ (2 Corinthians 4:6). So when reading the Bible the question that should *not* be asked is "What has this passage to do with the covenant?" Instead, the question that should be asked is "What has this passage to do with Christ?"

The Holy Bible is a book of progressive revelation. The sum total and final basis of redemptive truth was not deposited in the Old Testament and to think so denigrates the finality and glory of the New Covenant. Adam and Eve lived at the dawn of redemptive history and knew comparatively little of the light which we know today. They saw but the faint distant rays of the sun before it reached the horizon. Each of the covenants, as they were progressively revealed, shed increasing light in the minds of men about the truth of God and His great Christological redemption, which culminated in the noonday brightness of our New Covenant age (see 2 Corinthians 3:7-11). Anglican Bishop J.C. Ryle astutely makes the following wonderful and insightful observation:

> The difference between the knowledge of an Old Testament saint and a saint in the apostle's days is far greater than we conceive. It is the difference of twilight and noon day, of winter and summer, of the mind of a child and the mind of a full grown man. No doubt the Old Testament saints looked to a coming Saviour by faith, and believed in a resurrection of life to come. But the coming and death of Christ unlocked a hundred Scriptures which before were closed, and cleared up scores of doubtful points which before had never been solved. The humblest Christian believer understands things which David and Isaiah could never explain.[64]

The *second* purpose of the progressive administrations of the covenants is to narrow the redemptive field of focus. When Eve conceived and bore Cain, she believed him to be the one who would crush Satan's head, lift the curse, and restore paradise back to the *whole* earth. Alas, this was not to be. Instead of Cain being the Christ, he became a killer. Eve's expectations were crushed. Seth would be the one through whom the godly line would be established. As men began to multiply on the earth, wickedness increased with them. The LORD God distinguished Noah and separated him from Seth's line and the rest of the sons of men, whom He would destroy. After the Flood, God again narrowed the focus and chose Noah's son Shem, from whose loins would eventually come Terah and then Abraham. All the while, the sons of men continued to populate the earth.

Narrowing the focus even more, God passed by Abraham's first son (Ishmael), born of carnal scheming, and chose Isaac. Abraham's six other sons, born of Keturah, were not even considered (Genesis 25:1-4). Passing by Esau, Isaac's firstborn son, Jacob became the one from whom the covenant line would continue. Out of all the inhabitants of the earth, the twelve sons of Jacob and their descendants, the nation of Israel, were chosen to become the established covenant people of God

---

[64]*Luke*, vol. 1; (James Clarke & Co. Ltd.: Cambridge, England: 1976) p. 368.

on the earth. But, in the midst of the days from Sinai to John the Baptist, God again intervened, further constricting the focus. Not out of the priestly tribe of Levi, but out of the tribe of Judah (the Ruler), God selected David, the youngest son of Jesse, and made a covenant promising that from his loins would come the one Mediator between God and man. This One would have a scepter in His hand and would rule as the mediatorial Lord of heaven and earth. Much like an old western cowboy would drive cattle through a narrow chute into the corral, so Covenant Theology drives us through an ever narrowing chute so that the focus will ever be on Christ!

Here it must be parenthetically noted that not only is there successive narrowing and restriction but there is also progressive exclusion. Adam had many sons and daughters (Genesis 4:5), but God's covenant line was with Seth alone. Noah had two others sons (Ham and Japheth), but they were bypassed and God's covenant blessings were with Shem *alone*. Abraham's firstborn son Ishmael was a circumcised member of the covenant, but was excluded from the saving blessings of it. The same is also true of Esau, who although a covenant member was barred from its saving blessings. Jesse had many sons, but only David was chosen. *This underscores the very real point that every historical instance of covenant-making runs contrary to the theory that "covenant children" are produced by physical birth.*[65] One could be a true member in good standing of any one of the administrations of the Old Covenant, but still *not* be a recipient of God's grace and salvation. That is not the case in the New Covenant.

Israel, as the covenant people, would continue as God's Old Covenant people until the days of John the Baptist (Matthew 3:5-12) and our Lord Jesus, who together inaugurated the *final* administration of the Covenant of Grace—the New Covenant. The final narrowing focus finds that the members of this New Covenant would be those born of God through grace and faith, *not* those born into it through physical birth (see John 1:13, ". . .not of blood. . .").

---

[65]Paul states in Romans 9:8 that children born of the flesh, even though born to believing parents, are *not* children of God. They will never be so until they come to personal repentance and faith in Christ as Savior and Lord.

Herein lies the distinction. God's Covenant of Grace is now established with many different peoples of the earth far and wide from every "kindred, race, tribe and tongue," who are born of a heavenly, spiritual birth, instead of with the physical descendants of Abraham and Israel. However, the focus is still extremely narrow; it is *not* established with *all* of these indiscriminately, but *only* with those who savingly believe upon Christ (Romans 4:6, 13-17).

VIII. CONCLUSION

From the eternal counsel and decree of heaven before time began to the eternal state of glorification in heaven, God deals with humanity by way of covenants. The Covenant of Redemption poignantly demonstrates, in the Covenant of Works, why there is sin and evil in the earth and why there is a need for redemption. It progressively unfolds in history through the Covenant of Grace, which is administered through various covenants. Churches visible and local—which should consist only of true disciples who are baptized upon their profession of faith, who are knowingly and willingly covenanted together for the worship of our triune God, the edification and discipline of one another in truth and love, the proper observance of the ordinances,[66] and the spreading abroad of the knowledge of Christ as the Savior of sinners—are the final manifestations of the Covenant of Grace until Christ comes again.[67] Then, and only then, the

---

[66]Most 21st century Baptists, following our Baptist forefathers, have an aversion to using the word "sacrament" because of its associations with the sacramentalism of Catholicism and much of liberal Protestantism. They prefer to use the word "ordinance," thinking it better describes the true meaning of baptism and the Lord's Supper. Ordinance is defined as something ordained, a rule by authority; a decree. However, when rightly understood, the word "sacrament" (Latin, "*sacramentum*," meaning something sacred) is a good word and should not be avoided. Both words can and should be used.

[67]The question is sometimes asked about children of believers in New Covenant days. "Are they not members of the covenant like children under the Old Covenant administrations?" The answer is "No." It is true that, unlike children of unbelievers in the world, children of believers do possess many benefits attached to the covenant, such as hearing the Word of God, entering into public worship, being catechized by pastors and parents, having the influence of the church and a godly Christian home, being prayed for by the church and parents, etc. However, while they enjoy the benefits attached to the covenant, only regeneration and justification make them actual members of the covenant. [NOTE: Those who believe infant baptism places a child in the "covenant of grace" invent

immediate presence of God that was lost in the Garden of Eden, which was progressively increased through the various, unfolding covenants until it reached its zenith in the New Covenant, will be joyfully experienced without measure in the eternal state of bliss and glory (Revelation 21:1-3; 22:3-5). Worthy is the Lamb!

If one is to be truly consistent and biblical, then it is necessary to be covenantal. Baptists of the past and Reformed Baptists today, without equivocation, are covenantal and embrace Covenant Theology. This theological discipline helps us to understand the answers to many questions and enables us rightly to divide the Word of truth. It ever centers upon Christ and grace, which continually drives us to Him and causes us to glory in our Redeemer and in Him alone! And finally, it inflames and empowers us to preach this gospel of the kingdom to the entire world as a witness to the nations (Matthew 24:13).

Now may the God of peace
who brought up our Lord Jesus from the dead,
that great Shepherd of the sheep,
through the blood of the everlasting covenant,
make you complete in every good work to do His will,
working in you what is well pleasing in His sight,
through Jesus Christ,
to whom *be* glory forever and ever. Amen.
(Hebrews 13:20-21)

---

an unbiblical nether-realm where the child is neither lost nor saved; unless they hold to presumptive or baptismal regeneration.] Reformed Baptists dearly love their children and do not think of them as orphaned "second class" offspring or as little pagans. But they are not naïve enough to think their children are innocent or without guilt. They are keenly aware of the fact that their children are spiritually dead in trespasses and sins and are in urgent need of divine regeneration and conversion, which includes repentance, faith, justification and the forgiveness of sins.

CHAPTER 2

BIBLICAL HERMENEUTICS AND COVENANT THEOLOGY

Fred A. Malone

ℰVERYONE HAS A COVENANT THEOLOGY. Some ignore the covenants of the Bible and others overemphasize the concept of covenants beyond biblical evidence. Nevertheless, everyone has a theology about God's covenants in the Bible. Some Baptists tell Reformed (covenantal) Baptists that they cannot be a Baptist and still hold to Covenant Theology; other paedobaptists tell Reformed Baptists that they cannot hold to Covenant Theology and still be a Baptist. In other words, for Reformed Baptists to hold to Covenant Theology is controversial today.

So, who is correct? Non-covenantal Baptists, covenantal paedobaptists, or Reformed Baptists? As far as *The London Baptist Confession of 1689* (*LBC*) is concerned, English Baptists and their descendants in America originally were covenantal Baptists until the 1900s (see Philadelphia and Charleston Confessions). It was not until Dispensationalism spread among Baptists after 1900 that non-covenantal Baptists took the ascendancy. Now that Baptists have rediscovered Reformed soteriology in the last fifty years, it is natural that the question of Covenant Theology would reappear. The problem is that many Baptists who have adopted Reformed soteriology either have rejected our historical Covenant Theology or else have rediscovered Covenant Theology only to join the ranks of our paedobaptists brothers. So, can one be a consistent Reformed Baptist, holding to the Covenant Theology of the Bible?

I believe that we can. In fact, I believe that we must. Consistent biblical hermeneutics (the principles of biblical interpretation) drive us to be Reformed Baptists. At least, that is why I am a Reformed (covenantal) Baptist.

There is much agreement between evangelical and reformed Calvinists about biblical hermeneutics. This is why both of us have accepted Calvinistic soteriology. However, there are certain hermeneutical principles that separate dispensational Calvinists from reformed (covenantal) Calvinists. Even further, there are certain hermeneutical principles that separate reformed covenantal Baptists from reformed covenantal paedobaptists. It is my hope to identify these differences in this chapter and to apply consistent biblical hermeneutics to identify and justify the Reformed (covenantal) Baptist position so stated in the *LBC*. There is no contradiction in being a Baptist who believes in Covenant Theology.

A summary of the agreement between covenantal Baptists and covenantal paedobaptists may be seen in their respective confessions; (i.e., *LBC* - 1677, 1689) and *The Westminster Confession of Faith* (*WCF*). We agree that God decreed to create Adam in God's image as mankind's covenant head and to permit him to fall from the Covenant of Works which God established with him in the garden. We agree that God the Father and God the Son entered into a counsel of peace (the Covenant of Redemption) before the foundation of the world, making the incarnate Son to be the covenant Head of an elect people to save from their sins through His Covenant of Grace. Thus, all humanity falls under either Adam or Christ as their covenant head (Romans 5:12ff). We agree that after the fall of Adam, God instituted the historical Covenant of Grace in Genesis 3:15 with the announcement of the covenant Mediator to come. We agree that the historical covenants of the OT progressively reveal God's plan to bring forth the Seed of Abraham and David to be born in Bethlehem as the only Mediator between God and man, thus establishing the New Covenant as the fulfillment of the OT promises of covenant grace. We agree that all men live either condemned under the Covenant of Works in Adam or saved under the Covenant of Grace in Christ, awaiting the final judgment of all men by Christ and the final consummation of that Covenant of Grace in the New Heavens and the New Earth.

This common agreement between covenantal Baptists and covenantal paedobaptists should bring recognition of brotherly love and charity between us against an unbelieving world and those who oppose Covenant Theology. This, in fact, can be experienced at the Banner of Truth conferences held in the United States and Great Britain. However, there remains a necessary ecclesiastical separation between us because of certain differences regarding Covenant Theology. We still hold differences about the definition and content of the New Covenant which affects our doctrine of the church and the sacraments (i.e., ordinances), no small things.

The reason for these differences is neither stubbornness nor ignorance. These differences exist because of the application of our hermeneutics to the covenants of the Bible. If we could come to agreement upon biblical hermeneutics and then consistently apply them, perhaps we could exhibit a greater visible unity on earth.

Therefore, the design of this chapter is to study biblical hermeneutics and how different hermeneutics affect one's Covenant Theology. First, we will outline the common hermeneutics between the evangelical and Reformed groups. Second, we will examine the distinct hermeneutics which separate evangelical and Reformed theology concerning God's covenants. And, third, we will study the distinctive hermeneutics which separate Reformed covenantal Baptists from Reformed covenantal paedobaptists. It is hoped that this study will confirm Reformed Baptists in their Covenant Theology and bring unity between them, as well as to clarify to paedobaptists why we differ with them. Whatever the case, we pray that we will glorify our covenant God for His faithfulness to His covenant promises for the salvation of sinners.

I. AGREED EVANGELICAL AND REFORMED HERMENEUTICS

There are certain principles of interpretation (hermeneutics) generally accepted and followed by most evangelical and Reformed scholars.[68] According to Bernard Ramm, the explanation of theological differences between evangelical scholars is not that of different hermeneutics but

---

[68]The Chicago Statement on Biblical Inerrancy and the Chicago Statement on Biblical Hermeneutics are examples of such unity on basic principles of biblical interpretation.

of inconsistent application.[69] If only we all could be more consistent! The following *nine* principles are generally accepted on all sides.

THE INSPIRATION AND INERRANCY OF SCRIPTURE

Although there are wide differences among evangelical scholars about the meaning of certain Scripture passages, there is wide agreement upon the verbal, plenary inspiration of Scripture. That is, both the Old and New Testaments are fully inspired by God and kept from error in the original autographs. Divine inspiration and inerrancy is the foundation of the Reformation's formal principle: *Sola Scriptura.*

THE LITERAL-GRAMMATICAL-HISTORICAL METHOD

Most evangelical and Reformed scholars agree that Scripture is to be interpreted: (a) *literally*, according to the ordinary meaning of words in current use, unless the text and context places a different import upon the meaning; this includes the use of lexicons, expert language studies, secular sources, contemporary use, etc., balanced with a thorough examination of how God authoritatively uses each word in Scripture. For example, Louis Berkhof recognizes that such etymological and contemporary use studies must depend to some degree upon experts;[70] (b) *grammatically*, with strict attention to the grammar of the original languages, including the ordinary use of grammar from secular sources;

---

[69]Bernard Ramm, Protestant Biblical Interpretation (Baker Book House, Grand Rapids, MI: 1970), pp. ix, 10, 224.

[70]*Principles of Biblical Interpretation* (Baker Book House, Grand Rapids, MI: 1950), pp. 67–68. Scriptural usage has the final word, but Scripture was not inspired in a vacuum. The grammar and vocabulary of the Greek New Testament were drawn from secular, *Septuagint*, and Koine Greek. To determine the meaning of Greek words in Scripture without referring to normal secular usage is to deny the human side of inspiration, including an author's education, personality, upbringing, culture, etc. Such a view would actually close the meaning of many Scripture words (hapax-legomena; one use words) and create a redefinition of many words which would change doctrine. Berkhof explains: "As a rule it is not advisable that the interpreter should indulge very much in etymological investigations. This work is extremely difficult, and can, ordinarily, best be left to the specialists. Moreover, the etymological meaning of a word does not always shed light on its current signification. At the same time, it is advisable that the expositor of Scripture take notice of the established etymology of a word since it may help to determine its real meaning and may illumine it in a surprising manner."

this also includes the use of etymology and the current use of words mentioned above; and (c) *historically*, with regard to the historical backgrounds of the text; this includes the secular and biblical resources that enlighten historical events, customs, language usage, etc. This contributes to biblical theology, the study of texts in their historical context as God progressively revealed Himself in history, thus inhibiting reading our theology back into the text by isogesis.

Though agreeing on these things, sincere scholars still differ on how the Scripture interprets itself literally, especially in regard to prophecy and fulfillment, typology, parables, metaphors, etc. It will be seen in the second section that reformed hermeneutics adds one more principle to the literal-grammatical-historical method which is often rejected or diminished by dispensational evangelicals. This is the *analogia fidei*, "the analogy of faith" which characterized Reformation theology. It is more than the *analogia Scriptura*, "Scripture interprets Scripture." It means that the overall theology of Scripture, the whole counsel of God, must be involved in the final interpretation of particular texts and contexts of Scripture. Berkhof calls this the grammatical-historical-*theological* method of the Reformed faith.

<h2 style="text-align:center">SCRIPTURE INTERPRETS SCRIPTURE</h2>

This is sometimes called the *analogia Scriptura,* "the analogy of Scripture." This means that the final authoritative interpreter of a specific Scripture is the rest of Scripture. Most agree to this in principle. If a passage is unclear, other Scriptures more clear should interpret the passage. Scripture is its own best interpreter. Verbal and topical parallels to the text must be consulted for a proper interpretation of the text.

<h2 style="text-align:center">THE PERSPICUITY OF SCRIPTURE</h2>

This means that Scripture is sufficiently clear upon essential matters of faith and practice, even in modern language translations, to guide the common Christian in faith and life. This does not deny the need of gifted teachers to explain God's Word, but it does affirm that the Scripture is clear enough about the major doctrines of God, man, salvation, etc., that the common Christian should be convinced of their beliefs from the Scripture alone without blindly following respected teachers. As the *WCF* says in 1:7:

> All things in Scripture are not alike plain in themselves, nor alike clear unto all; yet those things which are necessary to be known, believed, and observed, for salvation, are so clearly propounded and opened in some place of Scripture or other, that not only the learned, but the unlearned, in a due use of the ordinary means, may attain unto a sufficient understanding of them.

THE UNITY OF SCRIPTURE

The OT and NT together are not contradictory but complementary, having the Holy Spirit as their common Divine Author. Both are necessary to discover God's will. This affirms that there is one overall message of God's mind as He inspired every Scripture. It is therefore incumbent upon the student to seek to understand God's overall message in the Bible. Most evangelicals understand this to be the revelation of Jesus Christ as Savior to man. Most Reformed believers understand this to be the revelation of Jesus Christ to man through the unified Covenant Theology of the Bible. This principle will be discussed in more detail in the next section.

THE DIVERSITY OF SCRIPTURE

God's progressive revelation in history (biblical theology) necessitates a distinction to some degree between the OT administration and the NT administration; otherwise the New would never have been given. God Himself said that the New Covenant is "not like" the Sinai Covenant in some way (Jeremiah 31:31-34). This involves the method of biblical theology which recognizes the historical progression of God's revelation to man. We must try to understand each text in the historical context in which it was given to understand its original meaning as much as possible before we examine it in light of all the Scriptures.

The Finality and Clarity of the New Testament

The NT is the final and clearest revelation of God to man and men must not add to it by alleged further revelations. This is not to deny that the OT was clear insofar as its design for the people of Israel. However, the NT is the final revelation of God to man in this age and claims to explain the meaning of what the OT meant (Luke 24:44-46; Matthew 5:17-20; 1 Peter 1:10-12). The NT finally clarifies and authoritatively interprets previous OT types and shadows (Hebrews 1:1-4, 8:1-10:32; 1 Peter 2:1-10). Some Dispensationalists do not accept this principle, which will be discussed below.

The Priority of the New Testament

Augustine's principle is summarized this way: "the New is in the Old concealed; the Old is in the New revealed." Because "the Old is in the New revealed," there must be a final dependence upon the NT revelation to determine how the OT is fulfilled in it. This is a necessary corollary to the concept of progressive revelation and biblical theology and is an essential prerequisite to a sound systematic theology. When defining the principles of interpretation concerning the relationship between the OT and NT, Berkhof offers several principles:

(1) The Old Testament offers the key to the right interpretation of the New.
(2) The New Testament is a commentary on the Old.
(3) The interpreter should beware of minimizing the Old Testament.
(4) The interpreter should guard against reading too much into the Old Testament.[71]

These are sensible principles to which most evangelicals adhere. However, it is this second principle, that "The New Testament is a commentary on the Old," that is often disagreed or inconsistently applied. Dispensationalist John MacArthur recently taught that the priority of the NT to interpret the OT brings disrespect to the

---

[71]*Principles*, p. 137–138.

perspicuity of the OT in itself.[72] This is a false accusation simply because biblical theology recognizes the progress of revelation to explain what went before, thus adding clarity.

The NT claims priority to teach how the Old is fulfilled in it as the inspired commentary on the OT. This is why the Lord Jesus Christ declared His authority over OT and non-instituted forms of worship (John 4:21–24), charging His apostles to teach the church to do what He actually commanded (Matthew 28:20). The priority of the NT for interpreting how the OT is fulfilled in it is fundamental to consistent biblical and systematic theology. For Covenant Theology, the NT explains more clearly how the covenants of God fit together perfectly as God's overall plan for man.

PRIORITY BETWEEN HERMENEUTICAL PRINCIPLES

Dan McCartney, a professor of New Testament at Westminster Theological Seminary, and Charles Clayton, explain that the meaning of Scripture is one and that no part of Scripture contradicts another. However, because men are fallible, some guidelines in the application of hermeneutical principles are necessary to identify those areas where the interpreter is likely to go wrong. They list five general priorities in the application of biblical hermeneutics:

(1) *The near context is more determinative of meaning than the far context.* A statement of Paul should be related to other statements of Paul before being compared to statements of Matthew or Isaiah...

(2) *A didactic or systematic discussion of a subject is more significant for that subject than a historical or descriptive narrative.* It should be obvious that when a historical narrative reports something as happening under some specific circumstance, one cannot draw theological conclusions from it...

(3) Related to number 2 is *the principle that explicit teaching is more significant than supposed implications of a text...*

(4) *Literal passages are more determinative than symbolic ones...*

---

[72] This was the teaching of John MacArthur at the Shepherd's Conference in 2007 during his message entitled "Why Every Self-Respecting Calvinist is a Premillennialist."

(5) Later passages reflect a fuller revelation than earlier. The most obvious application of this principle is that the NT takes precedence over the OT. Again, there is no real conflict between the Testaments when properly understood in their whole biblical and redemptive historical contexts, but the later revelation is fuller and clearer and occurs in our own redemptive historical context.[73]

All of the above principles are generally agreed to by many evangelical and most Reformed scholars. However, the next heading discusses the significant differences which separate reformed interpretation from dispensational interpretation.

II. DISAGREEMENT BETWEEN DISPENSATIONAL AND REFORMED HERMENEUTICS

The above presentation of biblical hermeneutics notices some differences between Calvinists of the dispensational and Reformed camps. These differences result in how one interprets the covenants of the Bible. This is especially true in how one interprets the New Covenant fulfillment.

Dispensationalists confirm the *analogia Scriptura*, that the more clear Scriptures must interpret the less clear Scriptures, but many do not accept the reformed principle of the *analogia fidei*, "the analogy of faith," that the whole theology of the Bible must be involved to interpret specific Scriptures.[74] This is why Dispensationalism places biblical theology as more important to the interpretation of specific Scriptures than systematic theology. To them, to include systematic theology as a part of biblical exegesis would be prejudicial isogesis of particular Scriptures. The result is a failure to appreciate the overall Covenant Theology of the Bible when interpreting specific Scriptures.

The problem with this view is that it misunderstands how to apply *three* things to the study of God's covenants: the unity of Scripture, the

---

[73]Dan McCartney and Charles Clayton, *Let the Reader Understand* (Victor Books, Wheaton, IL: 1994) pp. 195–197.
[74] Walter Kaiser and Moises Silva, *An Introduction to Biblical Hermeneutics* (Zondervan Publishing House, Grand Rapids, MI: 1994), pp. 193-210, 251-270.

diversity of the Scripture, and the priority of the New Testament for biblical hermeneutics.

THE UNITY OF SCRIPTURE

The unity of Scripture discussed above is based upon the truth that all Scripture is inspired by God. But it is more than that. The unity of Scripture means that all Scripture is inspired by the same mind of God so that there is no contradiction between one Scripture and another. There may be contradictions in our minds, but that is because of our ignorance, not because there is contradiction in the Scripture. Nothing revealed in the Bible is contradictory in the perfect mind of God and His eternal plan established before the foundation of the world (Ephesians 1:3-18). There is one message in the Bible, God's theology, which makes every Scripture subordinate to His overall counsel or plan.

But why is it not isogesis to include the whole theology of the Bible when interpreting specific texts? Well, the more you understand specific Scriptures in the literal-grammatical-historical method, the more it forms your overall theology of the Bible. And the more you form your convictions of the overall theology of the Bible, the more you understand how specific Scriptures fit into God's overall theology. Contrary to some opinions, it is impossible to interpret a specific text without any preconceived ideas that have been informed by your previous study of the Bible's teachings. For instance, if your exegesis of Scripture has convinced you that God has given different covenants in history, you may be tempted to interpret them as dispensations of different plans of salvation consecutively given, as Scofield did. However, if your exegesis has convinced you that God's plan of salvation has been the same throughout fallen man's history, then you will interpret the biblical covenants as consecutive revelations of that overall plan of God's grace for man's salvation. This is not isogesis; it is the consequence of exegesis for one's theology.

And this is, in fact, what exegesis has revealed:

> **2 Timothy 1:8-10** [8] Therefore do not be ashamed of the testimony of our Lord or of me His prisoner, but join with *me* in suffering for the

gospel according to the power of God, [9] who has saved us and called us with a holy calling, not according to our works, but *according to His own purpose and grace which was granted us in Christ Jesus from all eternity ,*[10] *but now has been revealed by the appearing of our Savior Christ Jesus,* who abolished death and brought life and immortality to light through the gospel, [11] for which I was appointed a preacher and an apostle and a teacher.

1 Peter 1:10-12 [10] As to this salvation, the prophets who prophesied of the grace that *would come* to you made careful searches and inquiries, [11] seeking to know what person or time the Spirit of Christ within them was indicating as He predicted the sufferings of Christ and the glories to follow. [12] It was revealed to them that they were not serving themselves, but you, in these things which now have been announced to you through those who preached the gospel to you by the Holy Spirit sent from heaven—things into which angels long to look.

It has always been God's eternal plan in the OT to prophesy the coming of the NT fulfillment of the OT historical covenants and prophecies in the New Covenant of grace. It was always God's plan to crucify His Son in atonement for the sins of Jew and Gentile. It was always God's plan to establish a new people of God, consisting of every nation, under the New Covenant fulfillment. The way of salvation through Jesus Christ has been the same since Genesis 3:15 when God promised a future Seed of the woman to save sinners. This is why Romans 4 and Hebrews 11 explain that the saints of the OT were saved by faith in the coming Christ while the NT saints are saved by the same Christ who came.

All of this means that God's overall plan of salvation was revealed progressively through the OT covenants (not separate dispensations) until the final revelation of God's covenant grace was revealed in the New Covenant of Jesus Christ. This is why no OT covenant (other than Adam's) can be interpreted as a different way of salvation. And this overall theology affects how we interpret specific texts in the OT in light of the fulfilled revelation we have received in the NT. This overall theology is the *analogy of faith*. It is necessary for the proper interpretation of each text we have studied through the literal-grammatical-historical method. The message of the Bible is unified and one. This is what enables the preacher to preach the gospel from every text without being accused of isogesis. Every text serves the revelation of Jesus Christ to man.

The *unity of the Scripture* calls us to study all the Scripture until we come to a consistent theology of the whole counsel of God which in turn affects how we interpret specific texts. For instance, now we know who is Abraham's promised Seed (Genesis 15:4-6; Galatians 3:16, 29). How can we now preach Genesis 15:4-6 any other way, now that we know that God has fulfilled His covenant promises to Abraham in Christ and His faith-seed? Now our overall theology informs the proper interpretation of this OT text. The proper hermeneutics which leads to a Covenant Theology of the Bible is the grammatical-historical-*theological* method. The *unity of Scripture* includes the unity of God's eternal plan when He inspired every individual Scripture. We now know this *analogia fidei* as the Covenant Theology of the Bible which is denied by our dispensationalist brothers. They hold to the *analogia Scriptura* which advocates Scripture interpreting Scripture by relevant passages, but they do not include the theological principle of the *analogia fidei* in their hermeneutics. The Reformed view is the grammatical-historical-*theological* method.

THE DIVERSITY OF THE SCRIPTURE

The diversity of Scripture sometimes has been used to deny a consistent Covenant Theology in all the Scripture. Everyone accepts some degree of diversity in Scripture between the OT and the NT. We all believe that worship has changed from human priests and sacrifices to the High Priesthood and once-for-all sacrifice of Jesus Christ. The New Covenant prophecy itself states that the New Covenant is "not like" the Sinai Covenant (Jeremiah 31:31-34; Hebrews 8-10). Christ established a new form of worship under His New Covenant (John 4; Matthew 28:18-20). There is diversity in the Scriptures.

However, even though our exegesis explains that there are differences between the Old Covenant of Sinai and the New Covenant of Jesus Christ, some take an extreme diversity between the covenants which favors consecutive dispensations begun and ended instead of affirming the unity of the covenants which progressively reveal God's overall plan. For instance, Genesis 3:15 announces God's plan to bring a Seed of the woman to destroy the serpent and his seed. Paul understood this to mean that the OT covenants were the unfolding of this overall plan of God. He calls the OT covenants "the covenants of *the* promise" (definite article in the Greek) in Ephesians 2:12. Some may refer this promise to Abraham's covenant alone. What about the covenant with Noah (Genesis 6:18, 9:9)? Was it not a "covenant of *the* promise" which was given in Genesis 3:15 as well? Was the Noahic Covenant not necessary to bring the Seed of the woman to be born in Bethlehem? Is this covenant not still operative in God's refusal to destroy the world by water again?

The diversity of Scripture does not undermine an overall Covenant Theology. Rather, it records the progressive unfolding of God's Covenant of Grace announced in Genesis 3:15, which was consummated in Jesus Christ and His New Covenant fulfillment. All of the OT covenants were progressive revelations moving toward that consummated New Covenant of Jesus Christ. They reveal the sovereignty of God over all history, the mercy of God toward sinners, and the faithfulness of God to keep His covenant oaths. Only an exaggerated or denied diversity confuses the meaning of the New Covenant. Let us hold to the biblical balance of the unity and diversity of Scripture.

THE PRIORITY OF THE NEW TESTAMENT FOR BIBLICAL HERMENEUTICS

The priority of the NT for biblical hermeneutics is sometimes overlooked by Dispensationalists in the formulation of the Covenant Theology of the Bible. To paraphrase Augustine: "the New is in the Old concealed; the Old is in the New revealed." In other words, one cannot fully understand the NT without its prophesied background in the OT. However, the NT reveals the meaning of the OT and how it is fulfilled in the NT. This priority of the NT to interpret how the OT is fulfilled in the NT has been rejected by some dispensationalist authors. Earlier, it was mentioned that John MacArthur addressed this issue in the Shepherd's Conference (2007): "[to make] the New Testament the final authority to interpret the Old Testament denies the perspicuity of the Old Testament as a perfect revelation in itself."[75]

MacArthur's argument makes no sense in light of the progressive revelation of biblical theology. Everyone accepts the progressive nature of revelation in the Scripture and that fact that subsequent revelation enlightens what has gone before. To state that the NT is the final interpreter of the OT does not deny the perfection or perspicuity of the OT for the purpose for which God gave it. Moreover, the NT regularly explains the meaning of the OT in ways that were not plain in the OT revelation, demonstrating its necessity for authoritative interpretation.

Our Lord applied this principle of the final authority of the NT to interpret the OT Himself on the road to Emmaus:

> **Luke 24:25-27** [25] And He said to them, "O foolish men and slow of heart to believe in all that the prophets have spoken! [26] Was it not necessary for the Christ to suffer these things and to enter into His glory?" [27] Then beginning with Moses and with all the prophets, He explained (*diermaneuo* – *"interpreted"*) to them the things concerning Himself in all the Scriptures.

Our Lord authoritatively interpreted the meaning of the OT concerning Himself to His disciples on the Emmaus road after His resurrection, as did Peter (1 Peter 1:10-12), Paul (Galatians 3), and the whole book of Hebrews.

Dispensational refusal to depend upon the authority of the NT to be the final interpreter of how the OT is fulfilled in it presents a stumbling block to adopting Covenant Theology. Some Dispensationalists deny that the New Covenant of Jeremiah 31:31-34 is fulfilled in the first coming of Jesus Christ, reserving its fulfillment in the future Jewish

---

[75] MacArthur's statement shows that he does not hold the priority of the NT to determine how the OT is fulfilled in it. Thus, under the argument of respect for the OT revelation, he ignores the NT statements to determine how prophecy is fulfilled under the New Covenant. This makes the church a parenthesis to God's OT plan and makes the New Covenant finally fulfilled to Jews in the millennium. This eschatology distracts from the importance of the local church in God's plan as well as undermining the doctrine of the Law and Gospel in evangelism and in teaching Christians to obey the Ten Commandments under grace.

millennium. However, the NT interprets the establishment of the New Covenant for Jew and Gentile in the first coming of Jesus Christ (Luke 22:20; Ephesians 2; Hebrews 8-10; 2 Corinthians 37-18). Dispensationalists reject Covenant Theology as the explanation of the overall theology of the Bible because of an error in their hermeneutics. The "progressive dispensationalists" have given more credit to the interpretative authority of the NT for the meaning of the OT but still do not accept the New Covenant as fulfilled in the first coming of Jesus Christ and the eternal plan to establish His church. This error necessarily separates the Dispensationalist and Reformed churches from visible unity and ministerial service.

While professing to believe in the *analogia Scriptura*, that Scripture interprets Scripture, the Dispensationalist does not allow the Scripture to establish that the NT as the final interpreter of how the OT is fulfilled in it. Thus, they reject the *analogia fidei*, the analogy of faith, which describes the overall theology of the Scripture as covenantal. In so doing, they reduce the unity of Scripture for an exaggerated diversity of Scripture. May God grant them to see the unity of the covenants of the Scripture to understand the full implications of the appearance of Jesus Christ on earth to establish His New Covenant in the church of Jews and Gentiles as the new people of God (Ephesians 2:11-22).

III. DISAGREEMENT BETWEEN REFORMED BAPTIST AND REFORMED PAEDOBAPTIST HERMENEUTICS

Having explained the hermeneutical disagreements that Reformed covenantalists of all kinds have with non-covenantal Dispensationalists, let us now explain the hermeneutical differences which Reformed Baptists have with their paedobaptist brethren. And, let us retain a charity that each is following their understanding of biblical principles with good conscience.

The main hermeneutical principle with which we all agree is this: *the priority of the NT to interpret how the OT is fulfilled in it.* However, Reformed Baptists believe that they follow this principle with greater consistency to form their Covenant Theology, which results in a different understanding of the fulfillment of the New Covenant in this age and its application to our distinctive ecclesiology. This results in a belief in the baptism of disciples *alone* and the concept of the local church as a body of professing disciples, rather than a body of believers and their children, who are entitled to infant baptism. It is this ecclesiological difference, which is based upon our different understanding of the Covenant Theology of the Bible that creates the disagreement.

There are at least three areas of disagreement between Reformed Baptists and Reformed paedobaptists in their hermeneutical approach to the Covenant Theology of the Bible: (1) our hermeneutical approach to defining a covenant and its content; (2) our understanding of the establishment of the New Covenant by Jesus Christ; and (3) our understanding of the local church and its sacraments. These differences are enough to separate us ecclesiastically while we accept each other as sincere brethren in Christ.

DIFFERENCE IN HERMENEUTICAL APPROACH
TO DEFINING A COVENANT AND ITS CONTENT

Earlier scholars like Johannes Cocceius and Herman Witsius defined a "covenant" in terms of a contract, an agreement between two or more persons. This caused a robust discussion among budding covenant theologians about whether the covenants of the Bible are conditional or unconditional, whether all have blessings and curses attached. This brought forth further disagreement about (1) the nature of the Sinai Covenant as being a covenant of works or of grace, (2) the role of the Moral Law (Ten Commandments) in evangelism and sanctification, (3) the membership of the New Covenant and local church (disciples alone versus believers and their children), and (4) the breakableness of the New Covenant by its members. Different views existed among Puritan worthies about some of these issues. The *WCF* and *The Savoy Declaration* outlined a mediating view about these differences.

John Owen took the position that the word "covenant" (Hebrew, *"berit"*; Greek, *"diatheke"*) means at root a promise, oath, or bond. However, each historical covenant must be determined by its revelation in context instead of trying to make all covenants either conditional or

78

unconditional. Owen felt that the conflation of all covenant elements into one overall definition for every covenant (Cocceius and Witsius) is a violation of biblical hermeneutics. He conceived the New Covenant to be an effectual and unbreakable covenant for its true members. Baptists followed Owen's hermeneutic as is attested by Nehemiah Coxe's inclusion of Owen's exposition of Hebrews 8-10 in his book, *Covenant Theology from Adam to Christ* (Coxe was likely the main author of the *LBC*). This definition of a covenant and its content marks a difference between most paedobaptist covenantalists and Reformed Baptist covenantalists. Owen remained a paedobaptist but his Baptist friends followed his hermeneutics to the end.

In the twentieth century, the definition of a divine covenant has arisen again among the Reformed camps. Some have defined a biblical covenant in terms of the ancient suzerainty covenants between kings and their subject nations. This would make each biblical covenant (like the Sinai Covenant) to have conditions for the subjects to fulfill lest they come under the curse and punishment of a broken covenant. Applied to the New Covenant of Jesus Christ, this model would define it as a suzerainty covenant given by God to man, to which man must fulfill certain conditions or else be punished for breaking the covenant. Others present the Adamic Covenant of Works model as a graciously given covenant requiring man's obedience to fulfill the covenant or else experience the curse. This idea of grace in the Adamic Covenant becomes the model for all divine covenants, including blessings for obedience and curses for disobedience. Therefore, this view assumes that all covenants, including the New Covenant, are gracious, conditional, and breakable. This has been a driving idea behind the rise of the New Perspective on Paul and neonomian views proposed by the Federal Vision theology which has plagued our paedobaptist brethren. In this view, the New Covenant is entered by baptism (infant or adult) which results in a covenantal election and justification, both of which may be lost if one does not continue in the covenant by non-meritorious works to the end, whereby final justification is affirmed at the judgment seat. This view denies the once-for-all nature of forensic (legal) justification by faith alone which has been a hallmark of historic Covenant Theology (Romans 5:1-2).

Other paedobaptist definitions of a covenant include O. Palmer Robertson's description of a covenant as "a bond in blood sovereignly administered." Robertson is trying to emphasize the fact that *diatheke* in the NT describes a divine covenant as a unilateral oath or "testament" of God to his subjects, sealed by blood. This is certainly an improvement over the older contract or suzerainty ideas. It also allows for each covenant's content to be determined by contextual revelation instead of assumed elements from other covenants. However, even with this improvement, Robertson transfers the organic idea of "believers and their seed" from the Abrahamic Covenant into the New Covenant, thus inferring the legitimacy of infant baptism by including the children of believers in the New Covenant. This inclusion of children is necessitated by calling the Abrahamic Covenant "the Covenant of Grace" itself instead of a "covenant of *the* promise" which is fulfilled in the New Covenant of Jesus Christ. This inference from the Abrahamic Covenant into the New Covenant violates the hermeneutical principle of relying on the NT to interpret how the OT is fulfilled in it (Galatians 3:16, 26-29).

Further, the New Covenant membership is defined in Jeremiah 31:31-34 and the NT explanation (Hebrews 8-10) as those who receive the law (the Ten Words in historical context) written upon the heart (regeneration), the forgiveness of sins (justification), and the personal knowledge of God (reconciliation). This separates the New Covenant fulfillment of the promised Covenant of Grace from the Abrahamic Covenant which included the organic seed of Abraham who mostly were unregenerate. To infer the organic idea from the Abrahamic Covenant into the New Covenant is a violation of biblical theology and contextual exegesis. This is why such luminaries as B.B. Warfield and John Murray claim the authority for infant baptism to be found "by good and necessary consequences" from the OT. This violates the final authority and clarity of the NT.

Following the same hermeneutic as John Owen's model, Baptists have defined a covenant as an oath, bond, or promise of God whereby man may be blessed.[76] In other words, each divine covenant is a promise of God to man, the content of which must be determined by the revelation

---

[76] See Chantry's chapters on Covenant Theology for a fuller explanation of this view.

explaining each covenant. Reformed Baptists are careful not to expand the definition and content of a biblical covenant "by good and necessary consequence" when Scripture defines each covenant by its own content. This separates us from our Reformed paedobaptist brethren on Covenant Theology because of our hermeneutics.

Reformed Baptists look upon the OT covenants as progressive "covenants of *the* promise" fulfilled in the effectual and unbreakable New Covenant, so defined by NT Scripture. Thus, "the New is in the Old concealed; the Old is in the New revealed."

THE REFORMED BAPTIST VIEW OF THE ESTABLISHMENT OF THE NEW COVENANT BY JESUS CHRIST

Reformed Baptists believe that the New Covenant was established by Jesus Christ in His first coming, is continuing in its fulfillment, and will be consummated in its fullest measure at the return of Christ in the New Heavens and the New Earth. This means that we believe that the New Covenant elements of regeneration, justification, and reconciliation were instituted for each New Covenant member at the time of its institution by Jesus Christ. This further means that each New Covenant member is born again by the Holy Spirit into the New Covenant kingdom of God (John 1:12-13, 3:3, 5)), that each New Covenant member is justified by faith alone unto the forgiveness of sins (Romans 5:1-2), and that each New Covenant member is effectually reconciled to God as an adopted child of God forever (Galatians 4:4-6).

This means that the universal church of the firstborn enrolled in heaven is saved by the effectual nature of Jesus' New Covenant atonement and the effectual application of that atonement by the Holy Spirit's regeneration. Both the saints of the OT and the NT are saved by the New Covenant's accomplishment of the eternal Covenant of Redemption which was announced in the historical inauguration of the Covenant of Grace in Genesis. 3:15.

However, the New Covenant local (visible) church is to be established upon a good confession of repentance and faith in Jesus Christ as evidence of the regeneration of the New Covenant. Although paedobaptists and Reformed Baptists alike may have unregenerate members in a local church, the Reformed Baptist goal is to build a church of regenerate New Covenant members. This New Covenant definition of the regenerate rejects the automatic inclusion of the children of believers in the local church until they yield a good profession of repentance and faith just like their parents. This is, in fact, how the first church at Jerusalem was formed (Matthew 28:18-20; Acts 2:38-42). Only professing disciples of Jesus Christ, who received Peter's words, were baptized as New Covenant members of the Jerusalem church.

Paedobaptists reject this Reformed Baptist view of the effectual membership in the New Covenant as the basis for a professing church membership. Richard Pratt has argued that the New Covenant will be effectual in every member in its eschatological fulfillment in glory. However, he says, it is now instituted with believers and their children and continues that way until the consummation of all things. The main problem with this construction is that God's previous covenants established the covenant and its membership as effective in the historical contexts in which they were given. Noah and his family entered the ark, Abraham and his male descendants were circumcised into his covenant, physical Israel as a whole entered the Sinai Covenant when it was given. When Jesus established the New Covenant in His blood, the regenerate membership was established as well (Jeremiah 31:31-34; John 3:5; Acts 2:41). All baptized disciples were assumed to be regenerate until they should prove to be false members by their apostasy (Matthew 7:23; "I never knew you"). John testified the false membership of professing apostates in these words in 1 John 2:19, "They went out from us, *but they were not [really] of us*; for if they had been of us, they would have remained with us; but [they went out], so that it would be shown that they all are not of us." John's description of apostates reveals that though some were members of the local church by profession, they never were members of the effectual New Covenant.

Therefore, Reformed Baptists have a different view from Reformed paedobaptists of the membership of the New Covenant, which establishes their concept of local church membership. Our Covenant Theology is informed by the priority of the NT to interpret how the

OT is fulfilled in it. We do not infer New Covenant membership to include the children of believers by "good and necessary consequence" as do our paedobaptist brothers. Thus, Baptists can be and have been covenant theologians in their unique explanation of the New Covenant and its application in the membership of the local church. The visible church is to be made up of professing Christians and entered by the baptism of disciples alone. This Reformed Baptist Covenant Theology requires an ecclesiastical separation from our beloved paedobaptist brethren.

THE REFORMED BAPTIST VIEW
OF THE LOCAL CHURCH AND ITS SACRAMENTS

As outlined above, our view of the fulfillment of the Covenant of Redemption, historically instituted in Genesis 3:15 as the Covenant of Grace, is the accomplished institution of the New Covenant of Jesus Christ. This makes the ultimate *analogia fidei* over all the Scriptures to be the Covenant Theology of God revealed in the person and work of the Lord Jesus Christ, predestined before the foundation of the world. He fulfilled the failed Covenant of Works in Adam by His obedience and He made full atonement for His chosen people in the Covenant of Grace accomplished in His New Covenant (Romans 5:12-21). Therefore, both the OT and the NT must be interpreted according to the overall Covenant Theology of Law and Grace as revealed in the Scriptures. With all revelation completed for this age, we look to Covenant Theology as the whole counsel of God to help us understand the meaning and import of every OT and NT text. Having done our exegesis and biblical theology, we employ the theological interpretation to check our grammatical-historical hermeneutics of particular texts by the whole counsel of God.

As a result, Reformed Baptists form their ecclesiology upon the NT revelation of the fulfillment of those OT covenant promises in Jesus Christ and His New Covenant revelation. He commanded His Apostles to baptize disciples and to teach them to do all that He had commanded them (Matthew 28:18-20). So we find them doing that in Acts 2 on the day of Pentecost. They preached Jesus Christ as Lord, they called sinners and their children to repentance and faith (Acts 2:38-39), they baptized all who received Peter's words by their confession of faith (v. 41), and they gathered them together into a professing church body to devote themselves "to the Apostles' doctrine, to fellowship, to the breaking of bread, and to the prayers (v. 42)." So, the visible church was formed upon the confession of Jesus Christ as Lord and the baptism of those confessing disciples into a local body. These baptized disciples then worshipped together, observed the Lord's Supper together, and prayed together. In other words, the Apostles formed the church and its worship according to what Jesus had commanded them to do (Matthew 28:18-20).

There are mixed practices among our paedobaptist brothers concerning those admitted to the Lord's Supper. Those who admit only children and adults who confess faith in Christ base their admission upon the NT command to "examine yourselves" before one partakes. They reason that the NT revelation must determine who partakes of the New Covenant sacrament which has been instituted by revelation in the NT. However, those who admit their infants to paedocommunion do it on the basis of inference from the OT practice of children admitted to the Passover Feast. But why the different practice between paedobaptist brethren? The answer is that the former allows the NT to determine how the Passover Feast is fulfilled in the NT institution of the Lord's Supper at the Passover, while the latter allow the OT to determine how it is fulfilled in the NT. The difference between them is the different application of the hermeneutics they both profess to hold to. If only the former would apply the same hermeneutic they use for the Lord's Supper to the NT institution of disciples' baptism alone; then they would strengthen the ranks of Reformed Baptists!

Reformed Baptists hold to a confessional church, a confessor's baptism, and a confessor's Lord's Supper because of their hermeneutical principles which form their Covenant Theology, not in spite of them. Our ecclesiology is formed by the New Covenant and the revelation of its content in the priority of the NT over the OT. This also involves the regulative principle of worship affirmed both by Reformed paedobaptists and Reformed Baptists. The regulative principle is the outworking of the NT revelation which determines the content and practice of the New Covenant church. We both affirm the following (*LBC* 22:1):

> 1. The light of nature shews that there is a God, who hath lordship and sovereignty over all; is just, good and doth good unto all; and is therefore to be feared, loved, praised, called upon, trusted in, and served, with all the heart and soul, and with all the might.[1] But the acceptable way of worshipping the true God, is *instituted by himself,*[2] and so *limited by his own revealed will,* that he may not be worshipped according to the imagination and devices of men, nor the suggestions of Satan, under any visible representations, or *any other way not prescribed in the Holy Scriptures.*[3]   [1] Jer. X. 7; Mark xii. 33. [2] Deut. Xii. 32. [3] Exod. Xx. 4-6.

Here we see that the sacraments fall under the regulative principle of worship and must be instituted by God Himself, limited by His own revealed will, and prescribed in the Holy Scriptures. The elements of this instituted and regulated worship include "the reading of the Scriptures, preaching, and hearing of the Word of God, teaching and admonishing one another in psalms, hymns, and spiritual songs, singing with grace in our hearts to the Lord; as also the administration of baptism, and the Lord's Supper (*LBC* 22:5)." Baptism and the Lord's Supper must be administered in worship according to the direct institution of God's Word under the New Covenant. The NT has final authority to determine the content and practice of New Covenant worship in the baptism of disciples alone and the communion of disciples alone.

Our Baptist forefathers self-consciously recognized that the regulative principle of worship was foundational to their distinct ecclesiology as Baptist churches. In the *Appendix* to the *LBC* (first issued in 1677), the following statement is found:

> 2. As for those our Christian brethren who do ground their arguments for Infant baptism, upon a presumed federal Holiness, or Church-Membership, we conceive they are deficient in this, that albeit this Covenant-Holiness and Membership should be as is supposed, in reference unto the infants of believers; yet no command for infant baptism does immediately and directly result for such a quality, or relation. *All instituted worship receives its*

sanction from the precept, and is to be thereby governed in all the necessary circumstances thereof (italics mine).

Here our Baptist forefathers attempted to be true to the regulative principle of worship concerning instituted baptism and the Lord's Supper because of the priority of the NT for instituted New Covenant worship. To decide for the authority of paedobaptism or paedocommunion on the basis of "good and necessary consequence" from the OT is to violate the hermeneutical principle that "the New is in the Old concealed; the Old is in the New revealed." The final authority for the instituted and regulated worship in the New Covenant is the consistent application of the priority of the NT over the OT.

Summary

We have studied the general hermeneutics which are agreed upon both by many evangelical and most Reformed believers. We have studied the distinctive hermeneutics between the evangelical Dispensationalists and the Reformed. And we have outlined the distinctive hermeneutics of Reformed Baptists differing from Reformed paedobaptists. What we have found is that Reformed Baptists more consistently apply reformed hermeneutics to form their view of Covenant Theology and the resulting doctrines of the church and the sacraments.

Reformed Baptists hold that God and Father and Son covenanted together before the foundation of the world to save an elect people from their sins under Adam's failed Covenant of Works. This may be called the Counsel of Peace or the Covenant of Redemption. That this Covenant of Redemption designated the Son of God as the federal Head of an elect people and was instituted in Genesis 3:15 as the promise or Covenant of Grace. That the Old Testament "covenants of *the* promise" gradually revealed the fulfillment of that Covenant of Redemption in the New Covenant of Jesus Christ as the accomplished Covenant of Grace. That the New Covenant is an effectual covenant in the heart of every member, not like the Sinai Covenant, thereby forming a new people of God by the regeneration of the Holy Spirit through the proclamation of the gospel of grace. That the universal church, saved by the virtue of the New Covenant, is made manifest on earth in confessing local and visible churches of disciples alone, governed by the instituted revelation of the New Testament to form and govern their salvation, life, and worship.

The inclusion of believers and their children in the New Covenant and New Covenant local church is a violation of biblical hermeneutics, erroneously relying on OT covenants to interpret the content and membership of the unique New Covenant of Jesus Christ. Each covenant must be defined by the content of the revelation given concerning each covenant. The NT has priority and must determine the content of the New Covenant and how the OT is fulfilled in it.

For these reasons, and more, Reformed Baptists claim Covenant Theology as their own and encourage all concerned to examine the consistency of their hermeneutical applications that we may build faithful New Covenant churches upon the Covenant Theology of the Law and the Gospel, which reflects our understanding of all men condemned under the Covenant of Works in Adam and of all the elect redeemed under the Covenant of Grace in Christ. This is the *analogia fidei* which enables us to see all the OT as a witness *to* and promise *of* the coming of Jesus Christ and the NT as a witness to His glorious first advent until He returns to consummate all things (1 Corinthians 15:24-28).

CHAPTER 3

THE COVENANTS
OF WORKS AND OF GRACE

Walter J. Chantry

"And I will put enmity between you and the woman, and between your seed and her seed; He shall bruise your head, and you shall bruise His heel." (Genesis 3:15)

"In the sweat of your face you shall eat bread, till thou return unto the ground; for out of it you were taken: for dust you are, and to dust you shall return." (Genesis 3:19)

"Also for Adam and his wife the LORD God made tunics of skin and clothed them." (Genesis 3:21)

IT IS DIFFICULT TO KNOW who was the first to call the doctrine of the covenants "the marrow of divinity" (or theology), but it is a most appropriate observation. Without bones the human body would be an unshaped glob of flesh. Without theology the ideas of Scripture would lie in an unshaped mass. Marrow is at the center of the bones which shape our body, and marrow gives health to the body. So the doctrine of the covenants is at the core of theology, and the health of any theological system depends on its understanding of this truth. It would be nearly impossible to overstate the central importance of the biblical teaching on covenants.

In Genesis 3, we observe two very different covenants in action and in force at the same time. The Covenant of Works is not introduced for the first time in chapter 3. But all of man's hopes under the Covenant of

Works were dashed here. The curse of the Covenant of Works is declared in this place, and it begins to fall on Adam, his race, and his world. The truly amazing thing is that, just as the curse of the Covenant of Works is imposed, a new covenant is published. Promises of the Covenant of Grace are announced (Genesis 3:15) even before the curses of the first covenant are applied (3:19). Also astounding is the fact that Adam's next recorded deed was an act of faith aroused by the Covenant of Grace. "And Adam called his wife's name Eve; because she would become the mother of all the living" (Genesis 3:20).

The head of sinners was not despairing over his colossal failure under the Covenant of Works. Nor was he overwhelmed by the dreadful curse of universal death which was announced. Rather he was hopeful. He was filled with optimism upon hearing the glorious and precious Covenant of Grace with its cheerful promises.

The Covenant of Grace arises from the ashes of the Covenant of Works. As man takes his first step into the ruins of the cursed earth, he does so trusting in the Covenant of Grace. These events are interpreters of the rest of the material in the Bible. Genesis begins at the beginning—with the framework for understanding all the Scriptures. If one misunderstands Genesis 1-3, he cannot possibly comprehend the remainder of the Bible. Genesis 3 and its two covenants dominate the experience and history of mankind and will continue to do so until this old and worried earth is destroyed.

I.   DEFINITIONS OF COVENANT

WHAT IS A COVENANT?

The Almighty, who is infinitely exalted above His creature man, made man in a state of blessedness (or happiness, or well-being). What this blessedness was is not left to our imaginations but is clearly spelled out in the first three chapters of Genesis. One, man had life, both spiritual and physical. Two, man had knowledge and righteousness, being made in God's (spiritual) image. Three, man had communion with God, intimate personal fellowship with his Maker. He enjoyed friendship and nearness to the Most High. This is always true happiness for human beings: to live filled with knowledge and righteousness, in daily companionship with their God.

As man was made, he was mutable or changeable. It was possible for him to lose his blessedness. It became a matter of sad reality that man did in fact lose life (Genesis 3:19), righteousness (3:11), and communion with God (3:8). While man was still in a state of blessedness, the Lord set before him a way to continue in and to be confirmed in his blessedness. Herein is the heart of what a covenant is: *a sovereignly given arrangement by which man may be blessed.*

THE COVENANT OF WORKS

Man might have had life forevermore. He might have been kept in knowledge and righteousness. He might have been the everlasting companion of the Lord of creation. He might never have known corruption, misery, and the curse. The way for sinless Adam and all his posterity to remain in a state of well-being and to be confirmed in happiness (to eliminate the possibility of losing happiness) was based entirely on what man would do.

> "And the LORD God planted a garden eastward in Eden; and there he put the man whom he had formed. And out of the ground made the LORD God to grow every tree that is pleasant to the sight, and good for food; the tree of life also in the midst of the garden, and the tree of knowledge of good and evil" (Genesis 2:8-9).

> "And the LORD God commanded the man, saying, Of every tree of the garden you may freely eat: But of the tree of the knowledge of good and evil, you shall not eat of it: for in the day that you eat of it you shall surely die" (Genesis 2:16-17).

Under this covenant, man *must do* what he was commanded in order to continue in a state of blessedness. If righteous man was to remain happy, all hinges on what he *does*! If man failed, then the curse falls. If man succeeded, blessing would be his and to all his offspring. Historically, this divinely-given arrangement by which man may be blessed has been called the Covenant of Works. That name was chosen because its focal point was man's working. Everything depended upon what man did.

Some dispute using the term "Covenant of Works" because the Bible nowhere refers to the arrangement in the Garden of Eden with this phrase. Of course, neither is a host of other theological words found in the Bible. What is important is whether the doctrines to which the terms refer are taught in the Word of God. It cannot be denied that the concepts employed under the phrase "Covenant of Works" are found in Scripture. If someone prefers to call it the "Pact of Eden," it does not matter so long as the content of this "pact" is biblically defined.

THE COVENANT OF GRACE

When Adam sinned as the representative of the human race, and he and all mankind had thus fallen, the Lord revealed His determination to rescue a great multitude from a state of sin and from the curse. Our God was not caught by surprise when Adam rebelled. Even before the world was made, the Almighty had formed His purposes of grace. From all eternity, the Father and the Son entered into an agreement to recover God's elect from the consequences of the predestined Fall. For reasons wholly found in the Godhead, the Lord did not wish to abandon all mankind to the curse they justly deserved for disobedience under the Covenant of Works.

Therefore in the Garden of Eden, the second covenant was published. This too was a divinely-appointed, sovereignly-given arrangement by which man could be blessed (or happy). This second covenant, however, was a method whereby man, who had lost life, knowledge, righteousness, and communion with God, might regain these elements of his well-being and be confirmed in them.

The Covenant of Works was not a way of salvation. It was a way for the truly sinless and blessed man to continue in and to be confirmed in his blessedness. Never, ever, has the Lord propose a scheme of works in order for sinners to be saved. The Covenant of Grace is the only divinely revealed plan by which sinners may be saved. Genesis 3:15 indicates that all mankind in Adam had become the companion and ally of Satan. Man, woman, and their offspring had become compatriots of the prince of darkness. They were in spirit more like the devil than like their Maker. Thus the Lord declared His plan of sovereign grace while addressing the devil: "And I will put enmity between you and the woman, and between your seed and her seed; He shall bruise your head, and you shall bruise his heel" (Genesis 3:15).

Jehovah did not publish a new set of rules for man to carry out if he was to be saved. But the Creator asserted *"I will"* do what is necessary to divide Satan from fallen man. *"I will"* bring man back to My side to fight with Me against the arch-foe. The wicked one devised a plan to engage man in attacking the Lord. But *the* LORD will see to it that the Seed of the woman issues the blow of crushing defeat to the devil. "Salvation is of the Lord" (Jonah 2:9).

If fallen sinner-man is to be restored to and confirmed in blessedness, his only hope is in what *God* does for him. Man, under the Covenant of Grace, receives the blessing of life, knowledge, righteousness, and communion with God. But *God* does the work to secure these. From man's vantage point, all is a free gift. It is all of grace. Thus it has been called the *Covenant of Grace*. Its leading feature is free grace to man from God.

In the entirety of Scripture there are only two divinely instituted arrangements by which man could be blessed: The Covenant of Works for sinless man and the Covenant of Grace for fallen man. Both covenants are referred to in God's first communication to man after the Fall in Genesis 3.

II.   SIMILARITIES AND DIFFERENCES IN THE TWO COVENANTS
THE WELL-BEING OF MANKIND

Both the Covenant of Works and Covenant of Grace look toward the wellbeing of mankind. Both address the question, "What is the way for man to prosper, to be satisfied, and to experience a happy condition?" And the blessedness to which each covenant points is in many ways identical with that held out by the other. Both point man to life, knowledge, righteousness, and communion with God.

However, in one sense the Covenant of Grace leads to an even higher plane of blessedness than was ever envisioned in the Covenant of Works. For the way of grace is only through union with our precious

Lord and Savior Jesus Christ. To be the bride of God's Son is a pinnacle of blessing above that which Adam had in his created state. To reign with Christ and share His inheritance is more than restoration to and confirmation in the blessedness Adam experienced before the Fall. In Christ, we are raised above the angels in honor and blessedness. Union with Christ suggests higher intimacy and privilege in communion, knowledge, righteousness, and life, than Adam had in his unfallen state.

As described in the Bible, the Covenant of Works breathes a curse. "But of the tree of the knowledge of good and evil, you shall not eat of it: for in the day that you eat of it you shall surely die" (Genesis 2:17). This word from God implies blessing upon obedience but expressly states a curse upon disobedience. Such an emphasis upon cursing in the Covenant of Works is important, because under the scheme of works cursing, not blessing actually came to all mankind. Also, men must be warned that, if they do not flee to Christ for grace, they must receive the curse. "For as many as are of the works of the law are under the curse" (Galatians 3:10a). Meanwhile, the Covenant of Grace breathes promise: "...her seed...shall bruise your head, and you shall bruise His heel" (Genesis 3:15).

The Covenant of Grace has no curse. None who enters the Covenant of Grace can be cursed, for God will do for him all that needs to be done for blessedness. The Covenant of Grace does not need to curse anyone. All mankind is already cursed under the Covenant of Works. As a matter of fact, "There is therefore now no condemnation to them which are in Christ Jesus..." (Romans 8:1a).

MAN MUST BE RIGHTEOUS IF HE IS TO BE BLESSED

Both the Covenant of Works and the Covenant of Grace demand that man be righteous if he is to be blessed. The Lord Himself is the source of all moral integrity. It is impossible for God to sin. He is opposed to all sin. He loathes sin and is angry with the wicked daily (Psalm 7:11). He cannot look upon sin without retribution being given. His instinctive response to sin is "Depart from me...." When the Most High made this world, it was *all* very good (Genesis 1:31). This meant that all mankind was morally righteous.

Nevertheless, a being devoted to evil was given access to God's good and beautiful earth.[77] The serpent (Satan) beguiled Eve. He deceived the woman and made her a temptress to Adam. What was expected of Adam and Eve was allegiance and faithfulness to their Maker, but they joined in the rebellion of the wicked one. It was this departure from righteousness that forfeited blessedness for Adam and his entire race. Genesis 3:15 indicates that only a return to righteousness would bring back blessing under the Covenant of Grace. Then instead of their being at enmity with God, the Lord would make His elect at enmity with Satan.

The standard of righteousness is identical under both arrangements (of works and of grace). It is nothing less than the moral law stamped upon the hearts of all mankind from creation: "For not the hearers of the law are just before God, but the doers of the law shall be justified. For when the Gentiles, which have not the law, do by nature the things contained in the law, these, having not the law, are a law unto themselves: Which show the work of the law written in their hearts, their conscience also bearing witness, and their thoughts the mean while accusing or else excusing one another" (Romans 2:13-15).

No one can fully escape an inward awareness of this standard even when he rebels against it. God is unchanging in all His ways and His expectation of man does not change. His requirement for man is always an imitation of His own righteousness.

Adam was made upright—with a heart inclined to keep the God-given standard of righteousness. Genesis 2:17 gives the specific command, "But of the tree of the knowledge of good and evil, you shall not eat of it: for in the day that you eat of it you shall surely die." There is much more to this commandment than appears on its surface. A testing period was established during which man must obey to be confirmed in his righteousness. The focus of attention was upon a tree.

---

[77] Note carefully the wording of the author – "was given access." Satan did not, as an equal, overpower the Lord God and break into the Garden, nor did he stealthily sneak into the Garden without God's knowledge. God Almighty permitted it or the serpent could never have entered. Ed.

Theologians often refer to this tree as sacramental. It is symbolic of all the obedience which man's Maker expected of him. It represents all of the righteousness required of man. Had Adam ceased to acknowledge God as his God, ceased to keep the Sabbath, been unfaithful to Eve, become a liar, or coveted, there would have been a fall even if he had not touched the fruit of the forbidden tree. As a matter of fact, eating the forbidden fruit involved a breaking of all Ten Commandments in the Decalogue! Many of these are explicitly shown in Genesis 3. Coveting the fruit, desiring to be God, disbelieving God's Word, unfaithfulness of the man to his wife, etc., are all in the text as part of eating from the forbidden tree. The tree was symbolic of the standard of righteousness man must keep.

Scripture is repeatedly insistent on this point: the Most High expects perfect and perpetual obedience to each and every statute in His moral law. Deuteronomy 27:26 is quoted in Galatians 3:10, "Cursed is every one that continues not in *all things* which are written in the book of the law to do them." James 2:10 is emphatic, "For whosoever shall keep the whole law, and yet offend in one point, he is guilty of all." Genesis 3:15 shows us that if man is to be blessed under the Covenant of Grace, he must be set at a distance from all sin. Sin and rebellion are defined identically under both arrangements.

There is one great difference between the two covenants: When man was sinless, the way for acquiring righteousness was that man would provide necessary righteousness for himself. When man is a guilty and vile sinner, the way proposed for acquiring righteousness is that man trust in a Mediator to provide the necessary righteousness for him.

Genesis 3:15 gives the first gospel announcement of a Mediator who can provide righteousness for the sinner-man. The Seed of the woman will be bruised as a sacrifice to take away the sin and guilt of fallen man. The Seed of the woman will bruise the head of Satan to destroy his power over man in leading him to sin. But throughout, both covenants have an identical definition of the righteousness man must have to be blessed by God. Without holiness no man (under either covenant) will see the Lord (Hebrews 12:14).

PRINCIPLES OF OPERATION IN MAN

The Covenant of Works and the Covenant of Grace have diverse principles of operation in man. The two covenants operate identically *for* man. Both aim at the same blessedness for him. Both propose the same righteousness for him. But the covenants have opposite operations *in* man.

The great principle man was expected to employ under the Covenant of Works was: Man must work to sustain his own righteousness. If Adam expected to continue in and be confirmed in the blessedness he possessed from creation, his only hope was to keep God's commands perfectly, perpetually, and universally. This principle is called, in Romans 3:27, "the law of works." The great principle man is expected to employ under the Covenant of Grace is completely different. Here man must believe. This is called, "the law of faith" (Romans 3:27). Man must exercise faith in God's sending a Mediator (the Seed of the woman) who will provide man with righteousness which is indispensable in the sight of God. Faith in that Mediator is the only way that fallen, guilty, polluted sinners can have the righteousness which God demands before He will bless man.

The operative principle in the Covenant of Works is "do for ourselves." The operative principle in the Covenant of Grace is "trust God's Mediator to do for us." "For as many as are of the works of the law are under the curse: for it is written, Cursed is every one that continues not in all things which are written in the book of the law to do them. But that no man is justified by the law in the sight of God is evident, for, 'The just shall live by faith.' And the law is not of faith: but, 'the man that doeth them shall live in them'." (Galatians 3:10-12).

In one sense, nothing has changed between the two covenants. What is held before man in both covenants is the same blessedness. What is necessary and indispensable to receive this blessedness is identical in the two covenants. The Lord required perfect and universal righteousness in both. The definition of righteousness is unchanged from the Covenant of Works to the Covenant of Grace. But in another sense everything is at opposite poles. In the Covenant of Works man must earn *by his doing*. In the Covenant of Grace, man must receive the free gift from a Mediator *by believing*.

IV. IMPLICATIONS FROM SCRIPTURAL PRESENTATION OF COVENANTS

COVENANT THEOLOGY IS AT THE HEART OF CALVINISM

Where Covenant Theology is misunderstood or opposed, usually Calvinism declines very rapidly. The statement that there are only two covenants, one of works for sinless man and one of grace for sinful man, is another way of saying that the Lord Jesus is the way, the truth, and the life, and that no man comes to the Father but by Him (John 14:6). All believers in the OT, all in the NT, and we ourselves can only come to God as sinners in Christ.

There is but one method of grace for sinners. God does not have multiple schemes for blessing sinners. He does not frantically crank out covenants in reaction to human decisions, until one happens to work well because man accepts it. From eternity past, there was but one well-conceived way for sinners to be recovered. All covenants since Eden embody this one divine plan of redemption through a divinely appointed Mediator. Such Covenant Theology is a close cousin of Federal Theology. Federal Theology teaches us that God approaches all members of the human race and dispenses blessings and curses to each under one of two heads. Either what Adam did will determine your destiny, or what Christ did will determine your destiny. "For since by man came death, by man came also the resurrection of the dead. For as in Adam all die, even so in Christ shall all be made alive" (1 Corinthians 15:21-22).

If you are in Adam, in federal union so that Adam has served as your representative and substitute, then you must die. If you are in Christ, in federal union so that Christ serves as your representative and substitute, you will be made alive! There is no third head, no third arrangement. This is simply another way of saying that there are only two covenants!

It is this truth which must be understood, in order to comprehend the doctrine of Limited Atonement. When Jesus died He died for His sheep, for a certain number that the Father had given to Him (see John chapters 6, 10, and 17). He was the designated Federal Head or representative of the elect. Our Lord, in His life and on the cross, acted on behalf of a stipulated number of sinners. Therefore all who are in Christ will come to Him and will be saved at the last day (John 6:37). All who are outside of Christ (outside of the Covenant of Grace) are hopelessly perishing.

It is possible for individuals to believe in Limited Atonement while they do not understand Covenant Theology or Federal Theology. Yet those who do so have a vague and indistinct understanding of this doctrine. They would not be able to explain or defend it to themselves or to others, without recourse to Covenant or Federal Theology. In the history of the church those who hold to some system of truth alien to Covenant Theology, have tended to cast off the doctrine of Limited Atonement. It follows naturally that other doctrines of grace come under attack as well.

There are many who defend Dispensationalism and deplore Covenant Theology. These Christians have tolerated "four-point-Calvinists," but they become adamant in opposition to any man who adopts Limited Atonement.[78] Dispensationalists instinctively sense that Limited Atonement involves Federal Theology or Covenant Theology, and they are correct. The adoption of Covenant Theology will include rejection of Dispensationalism.

DISPENSATIONALISM BEARS THE SEED OF ARMINIANISM

The entire idea in Dispensationalism, that God designed many schemes for man's rescue and breathlessly waited to see how man would receive each, is an insult to a sovereign God. Before the world was made, God determined to save His chosen ones by one plan (Ephesians 1:4-6). The plan was revealed at the Fall in Genesis 3:15—the Covenant of Grace.

Dispensationalism flirts with a relative standard of right and wrong, because it envisions a God who sets up and tears down laws and ways

---

[78] Ed. Also called Definite Atonement or as most Reformed believers prefer—Particular Redemption.

to righteousness as almost whims. It is no coincidence that [older] Dispensationalists have frequently taught a second work of grace. They conceive of righteousness as a mystical experience after the new birth which is tied to no definite standard. Scripture teaches that there is but one standard of righteousness which emerged from the very character of God: "Be holy, as I am holy" (1 Peter 1:15). It has been a constant in the two covenants revealed from heaven.

Some have called themselves "Reformed," but attacked what the Reformed confessions of faith teach on Covenant Theology. Although they are not consciously Dispensationalists, they revive many arguments of that anti-Calvinistic school of thought. Surely they have not done so intentionally or consciously. Yet, what they have taught subtly militates against the doctrines of grace.

They would be horrified to realize that it is so. But it is the tendency and the inevitable influence of taking their teachings seriously and working them out to their natural conclusions. It has been an attack upon sovereignty and upon clearly defined righteousness. Covenant Theology is at the heart of biblical truth. Those who are its enemies may do great damage to the church of Christ.

GOD'S COVENANTS ARE PERMANENT

When God makes a covenant it is here to stay! Again, in Genesis 3, there are two covenants in force at the same time. Dispensationalists treat God's covenants as almost whimsies of the divine fancy. It is irreverent to suggest that the Almighty is whimsical. He never is. Everything He says and does flows from majestic wisdom. But the impression made under dispensational teaching is that the Lord God had an idea for the human race at Creation. He published that plan to Adam, but man sinned, and the situation on earth became unsavory and confused. So the Lord introduced another idea. This did not improve the created realm, and thus the Lord gave still another plan. The unspoken suggestion in Dispensationalism is that the Lord is always a step behind man, reacting to His creature's decisions. It further implies that God utterly depends upon the initiative of man. If man does not ratify the Lord's ideas with human approval, they come to nothing.

Their concept is that there was an age of innocence which ended in disaster. That was followed by an era of Human Government. Since this accomplished little, it was followed by a dispensation of promise, and so on. You are left with the suggestion that the Great Architect in the sky is ripping up one plan after another. He is crumpling up the old designs and beginning on yet another. It is back to the drawing board again and again. The OT is little more than the Architect's work room of crumpled up, rejected plans. The entire area is strewn with failure.

God's covenants are treated with this shredding-machine mentality in the writings of some who still wish to be called "Calvinistic" or "Reformed," but who have made vigorous assaults on the doctrine of the covenants. It comes through in their writings and speeches that in their view old covenants are now rescinded. They suggest that the only covenant that has any validation today is the New Covenant introduced by the Lord Jesus. All other covenants have been scrapped, they would say.

We need to take seriously Jesus' words, "Think not that I am come to destroy the law, or the prophets: I am not come to destroy, but to fulfill. For verily I say unto you, Till heaven and earth pass, one jot or one tittle shall in no wise pass from the law, till all be fulfilled" (Matthew 5:17- 18). The Lord God never swears by an arrangement with man and then cancels the treaty. When God makes a covenant, either every element of it is perfectly satisfied by complete fulfillment, or else that covenant continues to be in force.

The Covenant of Works was God's first attempt with men. It is an arrangement endorsed by the Almighty. Since He who cannot repent instituted this covenant, it never can be revoked. Genesis 2 and 3 is not an interesting artifact of ancient history, dug out of the sands of time to bemuse us as we think of a world that once was and is no more.

The Covenant of Works is very much in force today. Genesis 3:16-20 is an explanation of our present modern world:

> Unto the woman he said, 'I will greatly multiply your sorrow and your conception; in sorrow you shall bring forth children; and your desire shall be to your husband, and he shall rule over you.' And unto Adam he said, 'Because you hearkened unto the voice of your wife, and have eaten of the tree, of which I commanded you,

saying, You shall not eat of it: cursed is the ground for your sake; in sorrow you shall eat of it all the days of your life; Thorns also and thistles shall it bring forth to you; and you shall eat the herb of the field; In the sweat of your face you shall eat bread, till you return unto the ground; for out of it you were taken: for dust you are, and unto dust you shall return.' And Adam called his wife's name Eve; because she was the mother of all living.

This is a world under the curse of the Covenant of Works. The two most distressing, yet most obvious, facts of our existence are the corruption of human nature and the nearly universal death of all mankind. Even we who trust Jesus Christ taste and see the curse of the Covenant of Works.

Paul preached the Covenant of Works as well as the Covenant of Grace:

Wherefore, as by one man sin entered into the world, and death by sin; and so death passed upon all men, for that all have sinned: (For until the law sin was in the world: but sin is not imputed when there is no law. Nevertheless death reigned from Adam to Moses, even over them that had not sinned after the similitude of Adam's transgression, who is the figure of him that was to come. But not as the offence, so also is the free gift. For if through the offence of one many be dead, much more the grace of God, and the gift by grace, which is by one man, Jesus Christ, hath abounded unto many. And not as it was by one that sinned, so is the gift: for the judgment was by one to condemnation, but the free gift is of many offences unto justification. For if by one man's offence death reigned by one; much more they which receive abundance of grace and of the gift of righteousness shall reign in life by one, Jesus Christ.) Therefore as by the offence of one judgment came upon all men to condemnation; even so by the righteousness of one the free gift came upon all men unto justification of life. For as by one man's disobedience many were made sinners, so by the obedience of one shall many be made righteous. Moreover the law entered, that the offence might abound. But where sin abounded, grace did much more abound: That as sin hath reigned unto death, even so might grace reign through righteousness unto eternal life by Jesus Christ our Lord (Romans 5:12-21).

For since by man came death, by man came also the resurrection
of the dead. For as in Adam all die, even so in Christ shall all be
made alive (1 Corinthians 15:21-22).

You live under either the Covenant of Works or the Covenant of Grace.
There is none other but these two. If you have not trusted Christ (God's
Mediator for sinners), you are at this moment under the Covenant of
Works. All of us were born in Adam, that is, under the divine
arrangement made with the entire human race. At the judgment seat
God will demand that the terms of this covenant be fulfilled. Multitudes
are now living under the Covenant of Works. Only those who have
entered the Covenant of Grace have escaped the hopelessness of still
being in Adam, born guilty, and born under a curse.

Even the availability of the Covenant of Grace must not be
misunderstood. When the Lord spoke Genesis 3:15, it was not because
He saw with surprise and frustration that the earth was perverted in sin.
God did not decide to give men a second chance with some wholly
different alternate plan for blessing. Once the Lord had instituted the
first covenant, its terms must be forever honored. Thus the first
covenant becomes woven into the second.

Under the first covenant, man must have perfect, perpetual and
universal righteousness if he is to be blessed. Under the Covenant of
Grace, the identical demand must be met. No lesser obedience will be
accepted. Under the Covenant of Works the curse pronounced for sin is
death. Man sinned, and death must be the result. Under the Covenant of
Grace a Mediator must fulfill a perfect righteousness for men who
cannot provide it for themselves. The Mediator will also die under the
curse of the Covenant of Works in the place of sinners. The heel of the
Seed of the woman is bruised, "Christ hath redeemed us from the curse
of the law, being made a curse for us" (Galatians 3:13). He did this not
by abolishing law or by invalidating the Covenant of Works, but by
"being made a curse for us." He met all the demands of the Covenant of
Works. He fulfilled all its terms.

As far as we are concerned, we no longer seek blessings by our own
performance of the law. We are blessed only by faith in the work of the
Mediator. However, the work of the Mediator has direct reference to

the Covenant of Works and endorses its right to rule the affairs of men. When the Covenant of Works was broken, God did not rip it up and say, "Well, let's begin anew." Nor did He do so with covenants given to Noah, Abraham, Moses, or David. A covenant must remain in force until all its terms are met and fulfilled. Therefore, every covenant must bend to and comply with all covenants which have gone before.

WE MUST SPEAK OF BOTH COVENANTS

When we preach the gospel biblically we must speak of both Covenants. What the Savior did to rescue His people can only be explained in terms of the Covenant of Works. The emergency from which He rescued His own was the curse of the Covenant of Works that had fallen upon them. The Covenant of Grace is not a wholly other, arbitrary concept from the drawing board of an indecisive God. It has intimate links with and similarities to the Covenant of Works. It is only because of this entwining of the two covenants that we have anything to say to sinners as we preach grace to Christians! When we preach to those under the Covenant of Grace (what blessedness is theirs through the work of their Mediator) we have a vital application for the ungodly. They are still in Adam, not in Christ. The blessedness we hold before men in the Covenant of Grace is the very blessedness sinners have lost and forfeited all rights to in Adam.

When by the gospel we tell of the curse from which we were delivered in Christ our Mediator, we have a crucial lesson for all not under the Covenant of Grace. This is the very curse which hangs over their heads in the Covenant of Works. We must tell them that if God spared not His own Son, but delivered Him up for us all under the curse of the Covenant of Works (Romans 8:32), they cannot escape the curse unless they flee to the Seed of the woman and secure Him as their Mediator.

BOTH ARE AGREED IN THEIR DEFINITION OF RIGHTEOUSNESS

The Covenant of Works and the Covenant of Grace agree in their definition of righteousness. The New Covenant speaks of ethics with great emphasis. There are lengthy New Testament passages devoted to moral instruction. There are even long chapters of "do's and don'ts" (e.g., Ephesians 4:17-32; Titus 2:1-11; et al). This is not because by doing the works of the law (any law, given by Moses or Christ) we can earn blessedness. We lost all hope of success through working when we fell in Adam. Nevertheless, Christ died to make us zealous of good works (Titus 2:14). That is just another way of saying that God put enmity between us and the serpent (Genesis 3:15). He planted in our souls a love of righteousness and a hatred of sin. This made us enemies of the devil. The only way to oppose the devil and to please God is to walk in righteousness.

Righteousness described under the Covenant of Grace is precisely the same code of conduct prescribed under the Covenant of Works. If that were not so, the NT would have no message for sinners. God's Spirit begins to work grace in the heart by convincing men of sin. Objectively, the Spirit makes use of the law, the moral law, in this work of conviction. We do not preach to sinners some new law of Christ. They are not in Christ. They are not under the New Covenant. They have no obligation to obey the terms of a covenant that does not apply to them. Nor are they guilty for disobeying laws that were never theirs to obey.

But, the moral law taught by Christ happens to be one and the same as the law in the Garden given to Adam and to his posterity. We preach the moral law to Christians, but not because it is a vehicle of their salvation. Salvation is a free gift through faith in Jesus Christ our Lord (Ephesians 2:8-9). In gratitude for the free gift already received, the Christian must seek to live in righteousness all his days. It is an act of thanksgiving. But the same law is still the high standard which all unbelievers are expected to keep in order to earn blessing in Adam. The more a sinner sees of the code, the less hope he has of his ever keeping it. He must find a Mediator to provide active righteousness for him. He must find a Mediator to bear the curse for him. He must find a Mediator who can crush the head of the serpent and empower him to become holy.

It is possible to slip into moral law with the glasses of the Covenant of Works. It is possible to read NT ethical passages in this frame of mind. When the "law of works" and not the "law of faith" is in one's heart, all obedience is legal and not evangelical. For this reason we must understand fully the natures of the two covenants. Merely barring certain OT passages will not eliminate the spirit of the Covenant of Works from men's hearts.

IV.   A CORRECTIVE TO PERVERTED VIEWS OF SCRIPTURE

At this very point of moral law, a blunder of tragic proportions has been made frequently. It was made by C. I. Scofield and his dispensational followers. Down to this very day others have continued on the same path. As people read through the OT, they come upon the Covenant of Moses, the great covenant given at Mount Sinai. Exodus, Leviticus, Numbers, and Deuteronomy are packed full of laws and commandments. When Dispensationalists read Moses, they say, "This is the Covenant of Works." The identical claim has been made repeatedly by others outside the dispensational camp.

There can be no question that the Jews were expected to perform many "good works." But then so are the Christians, as evidenced by long NT ethical passages. If that were all that was meant by the term "Covenant of Works," we could agree that both Moses and Christ issued covenants of works.

But there is a contrast between the Pentateuch and the NT. In Moses there is a much larger proportion of and predominance of laws and ordinances. The OT laws are more restrictive and "oppressive." The NT has much more of grace and promise. Again, if that were all that was intended by calling Moses' covenant a covenant of works, we could agree. In Moses there is higher visibility of law and more rigidity than in the NT.

But both the old and the new Dispensationalists have something else in mind. They really believe that Moses was propounding a way of salvation by works! They think that Moses was really teaching a "Covenant of Works" as that term has always been used by theologians. They tell us that Moses' teaching was, "The way to heaven is by keeping the Ten Commandments." There are some very serious problems with this interpretation of Moses!

First, Moses was only a mediator. God revealed the Sinaitic system from heaven! It is one thing for the Almighty to tell righteous Adam to continue in and confirm himself in blessedness by means of his own works. But it would be monstrous and nearly blasphemous to suggest that the Lord came to fallen, corrupt, and helpless sinner-man and seriously proposed that he seek restoration to life, knowledge, righteousness, and communion with God by means of his own human works. Such a course would be mocking man by demanding of him what is not possible.

Furthermore, it would be contrary to all that God had revealed to Adam (Genesis 3:15), Noah, Abraham, Isaac, and Jacob. To them, the Lord had decreed that sinners be saved by grace through faith in a coming Mediator. To suggest through Moses a return to a covenant of works for sinners would be a new thing indeed and a complete reversal of Himself. Dispensationalists teach that through Moses, God urged the Jews to do what they should have known they could never do! Jehovah had given a covenant of promise to Abraham. It was a system of grace for sinners. At Sinai, the Lord wanted to see if the Jews really valued this system of grace. But they failed the test. They agreed to obey the voice of God and this landed them back under a system of works.

What a horrible representation of God and of the OT! If this interpretation were taken seriously, the whole system of Sinai likens God to a cat playing with a mouse before the inevitable destruction falls. If the Dispensationalists were right, then no one under the Mosaic system, not Moses, David, Isaiah, or any other Jew would be saved; for both they and God would have put them under a covenant of works. "Clearly no man is justified before God by the law ..." (Galatians 3:11). And they would all have been under the law, not grace. Such a view of the OT is ghastly, and is impossible to defend. Even Dispensationalists somehow ignore their own theories and find a way to get the OT Jews out from under the very Covenant of Works that both they and God swore they would abide by at Sinai.

When the Lord came down to Sinai, He spoke audibly with all the people before He delivered the extensive covenant through the mediator, Moses. His very first words were, "I am the LORD thy God, which have brought you out of the land of Egypt, out of the house of

COVENANT THEOLOGY: A Baptist Distinctive

bondage" (Exodus 20:2). The commandments only then were given. It is plain from the beginning that the Hebrews were not called upon to keep the law in order to gain God's salvation. He had already redeemed them (nationally, at the Exodus). His heart was already with them. They were to keep the commandments in gratitude for what the Lord had already done for them. In addition, the extensive ceremonies of Moses all point to a coming Mediator. This is obviously a Covenant of Grace, not a Covenant of Works!

Every biblical covenant after the Fall is revealed by God as a form of the Covenant of Grace. Not one since Eden has been a Covenant of Works. Never, ever did the Lord give a covenant of works to sinners as a way to blessing! None of the biblical covenants since Eden operates on the "law of works" (Romans 3:27). All have as their mainspring the "law of faith." Of course it is possible for any person to read the moral law in the OT or in the New and to live by the principle of works, not the principle of faith. Some did this in Moses' day. The Pharisees did it in Jesus' and Paul's day. It is done in our own day. But the Lord and the Scriptures nowhere require this of sinners, nor do they suggest that blessing will follow for any sinner who lives by the principle of works. He is bound to fail.

It is because all biblical covenants since the Fall are united in their major feature of grace and major requirement of the principle of faith in man that our confession speaks as it does. All biblical covenants (with Adam after the Fall, Noah, Abraham, Moses, David, New) are but varying administrations of the Covenant of Grace. They all embody the same fundamental principles as to the way of salvation for sinners— through trust in the Seed of the woman.

The various administrations of the Covenant of Grace do differ in many ways. They are diverse in the measure of the Holy Spirit given, diverse in the way grace is expressed in worship, diverse in the way righteousness is enforced in the civil arena, diverse in the visible organization to which they are tied, and diverse in the express details worked out under the moral law. Still, in essence they are the same. They all require of man the "law of faith," describe the same standard: righteousness, declare the same Mediator who saves, and lead to the same blessedness for man. They all express the same great purposes of grace.

Genesis 15:6   And he [Abraham] believed in the LORD; and he counted it to him for righteousness.

Romans 1:16-19   For I am not ashamed of the gospel of Christ: for it is the power of God unto salvation to everyone that believeth; to the Jew first, and also to the Greek. For therein is the righteousness of God revealed from faith to faith: as it is written, 'The just shall live by faith.' For the wrath of God is revealed from heaven against all ungodliness and unrighteousness of men, who hold the truth in unrighteousness; Because that which may be known of God is manifest in them; for God has showed it unto them.

Romans 4:2-3   For if Abraham was justified by works, he has something to boast about, but not before God. For what does the Scripture say? Abraham believed God, and it was counted unto him for righteousness.

Hebrews 10:38   Now the just shall live by faith: but if any man draw back, my soul shall have no pleasure in him.

1 Thessalonians 4:1-7   Furthermore then we beseech you, brethren, and exhort you by the Lord Jesus, that as you have received of us how ye ought to walk and to please God, so you would abound more and more. For you know what commandments we gave you by the Lord Jesus. For this is the will of God, even your sanctification, that you should abstain from fornication...For God has not called us unto uncleanness, but unto holiness.

Galatians 2:16-3:29   Knowing that a man is not justified by the works of the law, but by the faith of Jesus Christ, even we have believed in Jesus Christ, that we might be justified by the faith of Christ, and not by the works of the law: for by the works of the law shall no flesh be justified...Even as Abraham believed God, and it was accounted to him for righteousness. Know therefore that they which are of faith, the same are the children of Abraham. And the Scripture, foreseeing that God would justify the heathen through faith, preached before the gospel unto Abraham, saying, 'In you shall all nations be blessed.' So then they which be of faith are blessed with faithful Abraham. For as many as are of the works of the law are under the curse: for it is written, 'Cursed is every one that continues not in all things which are written in the book of the law to do them.' But that no man is justified by the law in the sight of God, it is evident: for, 'The just shall live by faith.' And the law is not of faith: but, the man that does them shall live in them. Christ has redeemed us from the curse of the law, being made a curse for us: for it is written, 'Cursed is every one that hangs on a tree': That the blessing of Abraham might come on the Gentiles through Jesus Christ; that we might receive the promise of the Spirit through faith. Brethren, I speak after the manner of men; though it be but a man's covenant, yet if it be confirmed, no man disannuls, or adds to it. Now to Abraham and his seed were the promises made. He said not, 'And to seeds,' as of many; but as of one, and to Your seed, which is Christ. And this I say, that the covenant, that was confirmed before of God in Christ, the law, which was four hundred and thirty years after, cannot disannul, that it should make the promise of none effect. For if the inheritance be of the law, it is no more of promise: but God gave it to Abraham by promise. Wherefore then serves the law? It was added because of transgressions, till the seed should come to whom the promise was made; and it was ordained by angels in the hand of a mediator. Now a mediator is not a mediator of one, but God is one. Is the law then against the promises of God? God forbid: for if there had been a law given which could have given life, verily righteousness should have been by the law. But the Scripture has concluded all under sin that the promise by faith of Jesus Christ might be given to them that believe. But before faith came, we were kept under the law, shut up unto the faith which should afterwards be revealed. Wherefore the law was our schoolmaster to bring us unto Christ, that we might be justified by faith...There is neither Jew nor Greek, there is neither bond nor free, there is neither male nor female: for ye are all one in Christ Jesus. And if you be Christ's, then are you Abraham's seed, and heirs according to the promise.

CHAPTER 4

IMPUTATION OF RIGHTEOUSNESS & COVENANT THEOLOGY
(An overview of Romans 5:12-21)

Walter J. Chantry

PAUL'S GREAT THEME IN ROMANS IS RIGHTEOUSNESS, in particular the righteousness of God. "I am not ashamed of the gospel, because it is the power of God for the salvation of everyone who believes... for in the gospel the righteousness of God is revealed," (Romans 1:16-17). The Christian gospel is about righteousness.

I.   AN INDICTMENT AGAINST HUMANITY

Paul begins explaining the gospel by telling us that "the wrath of God is being revealed from heaven against all the ungodliness and unrighteousness of men," (Romans 1:18). His point was not that if the people of the Roman Empire did not repent, that God's wrath would fall on them. His message was that the wrath of God was *already* active and evidently upon them. At a time still future when he wrote, God's wrath would be seen as the Vandals battered down their gates and plundered their cities. But long before this terrifying, destructive blow, God's wrath was to be seen in His allowing the Empire to wallow in moral filth and debauchery. He permitted the Romans to corrupt themselves and to follow every lustful desire of their hearts without restraint. This was the wrath of God in its early stages, already fallen as Paul's letter was written.

Precisely the same message is obviously applicable to the United States of today. We are not speaking of a message that the wrath of God will one day fall on America if we do not repent. Rather, the wrath of God has already evidently fallen on our land. God has given an ungodly and unrighteous America over to the sinful desires of her heart and to the most degraded behavior. Because our land has given up on God, He has given up our nation to self-inflicted miseries. His wrath begins to destroy with unbridled shameful lusts, depraved minds, and filthy practices too numerous to mention.

There follows in Romans chapters 2 and 3 a most powerful indictment of all humanity as unrighteous. All without exception "have sinned and fall short of the glory of God," (Romans 3:23). That is, no one measures up to God's own righteousness, which is His glory! How then can any sinner hope to possess the righteousness of God? The Almighty demands nothing less or everlasting, divine wrath will fall upon the deficient.

Of course, Paul has given us the solution to this vital question from the beginning of his letter to Rome. "The righteous shall live by faith," (Romans 1:17b). We can only be justified (that is, declared to have the righteousness of God) through faith in Jesus' blood (Romans 3:24-25). Faith in Jesus Christ is the instrument which receives the righteousness of God as a free gift of grace.

II.   IMPUTATION

Still, that is not the end of Paul's discussion. Because having the righteousness of God is all important to each of us, he is compelled to explain it further. Chapter 4 tells us that when an individual believes in Jesus, a transaction takes place in heaven. Paul uses the historic and biblical example of Abraham to describe what transpires when a person believes. A new word is introduced to explain the heavenly occurrence that gave Abraham the righteousness of God through the instrument of faith. That word is used over and over to imprint on our minds the heavenly transaction. It is the biblical doctrine of "imputation."

The King James Version uses three different English words to translate this word. They are "impute," "reckon," and "count." Because this one word, used eleven times within the chapter, is precisely the emphasis of the chapter, the New International version wisely uses only one English word consistently, the word "credit." The Greek word is a commercial term that all will easily understand by using the word credit. We understand crediting someone's account on a ledger or in a computer.

When a sinner believes in the Lord Jesus, the righteousness of God is credited to him. In the accounts of heaven, the righteousness of God is credited to believers. When, on the Day of Judgment, believers stand before God, He will check His heavenly accounts and will find deposited in their account the righteousness of God. This is the extraordinary good news of the gospel. By faith in Jesus, the righteousness of God is credited to sinners' accounts, or is imputed to them. Although this news brings great hope and joy and peace to our hearts as the early verses of Romans 5 express, this heavenly transaction raises a question. How does God's bookkeeping work? How can a just and fair God credit the account of a sinner with the righteousness of God? Is God an honorable judge in doing this, or has He *cooked* the books of heaven?

III.   HOW DOES GOD DEAL WITH HUMANITY?

On what principle has God acted in crediting a believing sinner with the righteousness of God? I have been sinful, not righteous. How can God change my account from a debit to a credit? How does the accounting system of heaven work? What is this imputation of Chapter 4? That is the subject taken up in Romans 5:12-19.

To answer the above questions, to explain how imputation can occur, to describe how the righteousness of God can be credited to believing sinners like Abraham, this passage focuses on a principle employed by the living God in His government of our human race. You are living in God's world. The Almighty made the world and made us who live in it. He sovereignly administers all of the affairs of our human race. At the end of your days you will stand before the King of Kings and He will judge you. The principle spoken of in this section of Romans is central in God's administration of humanity and will be prominent in the decision process when you stand before God to be judged.

It is of great importance for you to understand how God's world, and God's government, and God's courts work. If you were going into one of the courtrooms of the country in which you live, and you were only going to be an observer, it would not be urgent that you understand how the court operates. But if you were entering the courtroom as a defendant, it would be of immense consequence that you comprehend the basis on which your case would be decided. Some day you will be a defendant and God will be your judge. The principle of God's justice revealed in this passage will play a vital role in God's decision of your case. You must understand the system in which you live. You must be aware of the rules that exist.

Here we discover that it has pleased our Maker to employ the device of representation in managing His system of justice for us. He does not always treat human beings merely as individuals. In the greatest of all transactions that have to do with our human race and with us, God has dealt with us, not directly, but through our representatives. Theologians call this the federal system and we will show in Romans 5 the actual verses where this is being taught. The federal system is foundational to what our confession of faith refers to as the covenants. It is at the heart of what people refer to as Covenant Theology.

IV.   COVENANT THEOLOGY

The Lord of heaven and earth, in His administration of humanity, has appointed for us a head, or a representative. The representative is one of our own, a true human being who is to act for us before God in His system of justice. In other words, the Most High employs the mechanism of collective or corporate management. This is a fact taught in Scripture with which we must all come to terms.

We understand this on an earthly level. Some of the decisions which have the most far-reaching impact on your life are made for you by representatives. You cannot act directly in international affairs. You have representatives in Washington. When they make decisions, they are your decisions, whether you like them or not. If your representatives declare war, you are at war. It will do no good to cry, "I didn't vote for him and I disagree with his behavior in this matter." Your heads have plunged you into war with all of its consequences. We act corporately.

Some of you work for large corporations. It is not possible for every employee to sit down with the CEO or president of the corporation and to negotiate his personal working arrangement. There are representatives who conduct collective bargaining. Your future income and working conditions will rise and fall with the wisdom and effectiveness of the person representing you in collective bargaining.

This is even true socially in our families. If fathers act with wisdom in working hard, managing finances with skill, making educational and spiritual decisions with insight, it will have important consequences for their children. Very few children would have chosen the social, economic, and emotional consequences which they bear from their parents' divorce.

V.   THE HISTORIES OF ADAM & JESUS

In God's world, there is representation or collective bargaining. When the Holy One made the human race, He appointed Adam as our head. The Lord assigned Adam a test that was more than personal. It was a test for Adam and for all whom he represented. Adam was in collective bargaining for himself and for all who would be born of him by natural generation. The consequences of that test would have the most wide-ranging effect and profound impact upon every one of his posterity, everyone who was in Adam, and everyone whom he represented. It was God who set up the mechanism of representation and who appointed the representative. Adam took the test for us all.

In Romans 5:12, the Scriptures speak of this governmental arrangement: "Therefore, just as sin entered the world through one man, and death through sin, and in this way death came to all men because all sinned." This is an astounding statement that one man has brought sin and death upon us all. That is not the common thought people have as to how God is going to deal with us.

When it says in verse 12, "and in this way death came to all men because all sinned," it is not saying that all sinned because all did the same thing that Adam did. The proof that the verse is not saying that is found in verse 14, where we read, "Nevertheless, death reigned from the time of Adam to the time of Moses, even over those who did not sin by breaking a command, as did Adam." Some never sinned personally as Adam did, but they were in him, represented by him. He acted for them and they die as the consequence of Adam's first foul deed. Because of one man's one sinful deed, all are sinners. All are constituted sinners, all are condemned, and all are destined to die. Verse 18: "the result of one trespass was condemnation for all men." Verse 19, "...through the disobedience of the one man the many were constituted sinners." The entire passage is repetitious for emphasis that one act of the one man made many sinners and brought to the many condemnation and death.

The passage teaches that the most horrible realities of our human existence are all the consequences of the one act of one man, our representative, Adam. "In sin your mother conceived you," (Psalm 51:5) and "from the womb you have been wayward speaking lies," (Psalm 58:3). Your sinful constitution is the direct result of the one act of the one man in his failure of the representative test. From the first instant of your existence, you have been condemned by God because of the one act of the one man. From the time of your conception, death began to stalk you with the assurance that you were his as a consequence of the one act of the one man.

To be very blunt, God holds you responsible for another man's act. The Lord is not arbitrary about this. It does not mean that, when you stand before God and the books are opened, you will be credited with the sin of some unknown, distant relative. This mechanism of being credited with another man's act is only employed in the case of divinely appointed representatives. Adam was such a person.

There is only one other individual who has served in a similar capacity as representative for vast numbers of the human race in God's scheme of government. Only one other was appointed by God for collective bargaining with heaven on behalf of members of the human race. That other person is Jesus Christ. To show that He is the only man beside Adam to serve as a federal representative, Jesus is called the second Adam, (1 Corinthians 15:45).

Romans 5:18-19 clearly draws the parallel function of Christ and Adam. "Just as the result of one trespass was condemnation for all, so

116

also the result of one act of righteousness was justification that brings life for all. For just as through the disobedience of the one man, the many were constituted sinners, so also through the obedience of the one man the many will be constituted righteous." Because of the one righteous act of the one man, Jesus Christ, multitudes will be justified before God (declared to have the righteousness of God).

All who were in Adam were constituted sinners, were condemned, and were sentenced to die. All who were in Christ will be constituted righteous, will be justified, and will have eternal life. How can God credit the account of a sinner, like Abraham or like me, with the righteousness of God (Romans 4)? The answer: on the basis of God's great representative principle, of His governing the human race in a federal manner, of His administering humanity under a covenantal arrangement (Romans 5).

This is a great fact of our world. God governs the human race on a collective basis, under heads whom He appoints. Actions and decisions of the two federal heads are imputed or credited to those whom they represent. In other words, we bear the responsibility for what these representatives have done. In one case, the act of one man led to condemnation and death for a vast multitude. In the other case, the one act of one man led to justification and life for a vast multitude. Our lives are profoundly determined in time and in eternity by representatives. The histories of Adam and Jesus are not merely interesting curiosities of the past. They determine one's destiny. These two acted for us as representatives.

VI.   THIS TEACHING HATED

You can imagine that some people hate this Bible teaching with a passion. Those who have a great sense of independence and individualism want to stand on their own two feet, to be "captains of their own fate," to "get what is coming to them." Those who have great confidence in human nature and those who believe that, on their own, men can reach nobility, virtue or goodness, will deplore the idea of imputation. Whether confidence is placed in human intellect or human will or basic human moral goodness, multitudes will have nothing to do with a federal head determining their ultimate ends. There is a violent human reaction against God crediting one man with the act of another man.

It is complained that it would be unjust for God to view one person as responsible for another person's actions. That would be called unfair. This is not only the criticism of Christianity by unbelievers; it is the serious objection of theologians like Pelagius and Arminius, and it is the response of multitudes who call themselves evangelical Christians.

There are two answers to these objections. First, justice is to be defined by a holy and just God, not by a corrupt and criminally guilty mankind. Our Maker will determine how to administer this humanity; the creatures will not dictate to the Creator. Secondly, if it is unfair for God to condemn us for the act of Adam, then there is no vehicle or mechanism to save sinners, for it would be equally unfair to save a sinner on the basis of what Jesus Christ has done. The entire apparatus for saving sinners rests upon the same administrative principle by which we were condemned in Adam—imputation.

People are especially disturbed by the biblical doctrine of original sin. Especially in our democratic society people cry, "I didn't vote for Adam and I didn't ask him to plunge me into condemnation and death." However, when a sinner looks to the cross and discovers that he may have the righteousness of God credited to him on the basis of the one act of Jesus, he is delighted with the device of administration called imputation. Our NT rings with awareness of this representative principle: "As in Adam all die so in Christ all will be made alive," (1 Corinthians 15:22). In Adam or in Christ, there is no third category. "God made him who had no sin to be sin for us, so that in him we might become the righteousness of God," (2 Corinthians 5:21).

VII.   UNDERSTANDING COVENANT THEOLOGY

This teaching of Romans 5 and of all the Scripture has been called Covenant Theology. These two great covenants for humanity are described in Chapters 6 and 7 of *The London Baptist Confession of Faith of 1689*. Arising from passages like Genesis 2-3 and Romans 5:12-21, these two arrangements/covenants made by God with mankind's only two federal heads, find all of Scripture organized under them. The understanding that there are only two covenants or two representatives whose actions are imputed to all who were in them gives structure for understanding God's Word. There have only been two arrangements by which men might have the favor and blessing of God, one in Adam and one in Christ.

When God made man, He very clearly published the terms under which righteous man could continue to enjoy God's favor and blessing. Adam, our representative, was required to continue in righteousness under a test. Adam failed. His fall plunged us into sin, guilt, shame, and misery.

God immediately (Genesis 3:15) published a way for sinners, fallen in Adam, to have righteousness and thereby restoration to God's favor and blessing. It would be by the person and work of another representative, Jesus the coming Savior. This was by grace through faith in the Son of God, whose one act would credit us who believe in him with the righteousness of God.

Both of these covenants are in force today. The covenant in which Adam represented us has not been set aside and forgotten. All the arrangements of that agreement are still in force. People are born sinners, condemned by God and die because the Almighty is enforcing the terms of the covenant made with Adam. Unless people are savingly united through faith to Jesus Christ, the second and last Adam, the covenant with Adam will determine their destinies forever and ever. Union with Jesus Christ is a necessity because the first covenant has *not* been canceled by God. Again we return to the issue that God will deal with you under one of two representatives whom He appointed.

Scripture tells us of various historic covenants that followed His arrangement with Adam. He made covenants with Noah, Abraham, Moses, David and Christ; however, all of these are merely various administrations of the one Covenant of Grace in which Jesus is the appointed representative and in which men are saved by grace through faith in the Messiah.

When Adam heard Genesis 3:15, he began to look forward in hope to the Seed of the woman (Jesus Christ). The first words out of Adam's mouth, after God pronounced the curses for the broken covenant, were to call his wife "Eve, because she would become the mother of all the living" (Genesis 3:20). After the Fall, Adam, the patriarchs, Abraham, Moses, and David all trusted in a second representative, or covenant head, Jesus Christ. As time went by, the arrangement to have one act of one man provide the righteousness of God for believers became more and more plain—but it was one and the same covenant arrangement.

VIII. IMPUTATION & CALVINISM

Not only is the doctrine of imputation a key to understanding the relationship between the OT and NT, it is also the linchpin of Calvinism. A linchpin is a pin passed through the end of an axle to keep a wheel in position. For example, a tricycle usually has a solid axle on the back that holds two of its three wheels. On the axle, outside the two wheels, are small holes through which steel pins are placed and bent over. They are the linchpins which hold on the wheels. If a linchpin breaks or falls out, the wheel will fall off and the tricycle will be useless.

Historically, men who dislike Calvinism try to destroy that doctrine by cutting off the linchpin of imputation. Enemies have wisely discerned that if imputation can be successfully attacked, Calvinism will be dismantled and broken. Such assaults usually begin with a high appreciation of man-centered philosophy. All humanistic systems assert that it would not be fair for God to hold one man accountable for another man's action. Once that has been accepted, original sin or the imputation of Adam's sin to us is denied. Following this, particular atonement is overthrown and Calvinism is gone.

IX. THE INFLUENCE OF THE SCHOOL OF SAUMUR

In fact, that is what occurred at the school of Saumur, France, shortly after the death of John Calvin. Saumur was a French Protestant Theological School in which professors were greatly influenced by the

COVENANT THEOLOGY: A Baptist Distinctive

philosophy of a Protestant humanist named Ramus. A change in teaching took place within the school over a number of years.

John Cameron, a Scot, was teaching at Saumur. He began to make a distinction between man's natural ability and man's moral inability as he taught on the subject of the human will. This, you see, would exalt the will of man and exalt man's influence over his own destiny.

As years passed, other theologians who were taught by Cameron further developed his thoughts. A man named LaPlace attacked the doctrine of original sin. He claimed that it would not be right for God to impute the act of Adam to other men. Because French Protestants were virtually all Calvinists, he could not eliminate the word imputation. Rather he invented the term *mediate imputation*. His theory was that men become sinners and are condemned and subject to death *only* when they themselves sin. You can see that there is no imputation at all in his theory. Yet this is the most popular theory today among evangelical Christians. They believe that men hold their destinies in their own hands.

As LaPlace developed his teaching, alongside him labored Moyse Amyraut. You may have heard of Amyraldanism. Some think of Amyraldanism as four-point Calvinism, the view of people who are getting close, but have not quite seen all of the implications of God's sovereignty. Of course Amyraut did indeed attack the doctrine of limited atonement.

However, Amyraut was logically working through the humanism of Ramus, the exalted human will of Cameron, and the denial of the imputation of Adam's first sin by LaPlace. He developed what has been called theoretical universalism as his view of Christ's atonement.[79] By this process Calvinism was gone at Saumur. Realizing the import of the Saumur teaching, true Calvinists found it necessary to teach extensively

---

[79] Ed. note: This theory today is often called the Multiple Intent View of the Atonement. For a biblical and more consistent view of the atonement and work of Christ on the cross see *Redemption Accomplished and Applied*, John Murray (Eerdmans, Grand Rapids: 1955) and the quintessential treatise by John Owen entitled "The Death of Death in the Death of Christ" in *The Works of John Owen*, vol. 10 (Banner of Truth Trust, Edinburgh: 1967) pp. 140-471.

on the covenant structure of God's dealings with mankind, especially emphasizing the doctrine of imputation.

A parallel course may be found in American church history. All of us are aware of the godly contributions of Jonathan Edwards to the Great Awakening. Perhaps less known is the fact that Jonathan Edwards wrote a very scholarly treatise on man's will in which he used the precise language of John Cameron. He too distinguishes between the natural ability of man and the moral inability of man.

The immediate students of Edwards, including his own son, very directly attacked the concept of the imputation of Adam's sin to his posterity. They claimed that Edwards himself had led them in this direction. New England theology was then on its way. Man's will was elevated, and the principle that God can impute the action of one man to another was denied. Out of New England theology emerged unCalvinistic Presbyterianism, Charles Finney-style evangelism, and other tendencies that exalt man (especially his will) at great cost to God's sovereignty.

All of this shows that the doctrine of imputation is the linchpin of Calvinism. Some of you are very excited about Calvinism. You love the truths of Sovereign Grace in the salvation of man. But why do churches give up Calvinism after it has been taught to them? Over and over again it is assaulted over the issue of imputation and the system of Covenant Theology.

X.   ONE FURTHER IMPLICATION

There is one further implication of Romans 5:12-21 that must be mentioned. Imputation is the keystone of the biblical doctrine of substitutionary atonement. What is a keystone? It is the topmost stone in an arch. As an arch comes together at its center, there is one stone (a keystone) upon which both sides of the arch lean. Everything that has to do with substitutionary atonement leans on the doctrine of imputation. Remove the keystone and all will collapse.

This is what Paul had been saying in Romans. In 4:25 we are told that Christ "was delivered over to death for our sins and was raised to life for our justification." This message required a discussion of imputation in Chapter 5. Jesus was held accountable for our sins. We are credited with his act on the cross. That is how we receive the righteousness of God! When, for any reason, the biblical teaching of God's crediting one man for another man's actions is attacked, the very idea of substitutionary atonement is under attack. If such attacks are carried to their necessary and logical conclusions, the biblical ideas of the atonement will disappear.

Limited atonement is the only view that consistently and faithfully defends substitutionary atonement. Limited atonement speaks more about the nature of the atonement than about its extent. The two questions are always mutually influencing. If you do not like the idea of one man actually representing other individuals who are credited with his acts, then you must define Jesus on the cross as something other than a substitute.

In fact, Saumur's theology and New England theology eventually redefined the nature of the atonement! If you exalt the will of man, atonement will suffer. If you deny the imputation of Adam's sin, suggesting that Adam was only an influence on others, and that men are condemned only for their own sins, you will redefine the cross. Soon you will not like hymns that say, "bearing shame and scoffing rude, in my place condemned he stood, sealed my pardon with his blood..." Eventually those who deny imputation will deny Christ suffering as our substitute.

Biblical doctrines rely on one another and influence each other. The history of the church has shown that an attack on one teaching will affect other teachings. The Book of Romans explains to us the gospel of Jesus Christ. This matter of imputation is very central to understanding the transactions by which we are saved. Its denial will have catastrophic consequences for understanding the Scriptures, for the doctrines of grace, and for the atonement we hold so dear.

CHAPTER 5

BAPTISM AND COVENANT THEOLOGY

Walter J. Chantry

No BAPTIST BEGINS TO SEEK AN ANSWER to the question "Who should be baptized?" by studying the Bible's doctrine of the covenants. Rather, he begins with New Testament texts which deal directly with the term "baptize." In a later study of Covenant Theology, he finds confirmation and undergirding of his conclusions.

NEW TESTAMENT BAPTISM DEFINED

In the NT, we discover the nature of baptism defined. In the definition, something must be said about the person baptized. Its central significance is that the one baptized is said to be savingly joined to Christ. We agree that the definition in *The Westminster Confession of Faith* is essentially biblical:

> Baptism is a sacrament of the New Testament, ordained by Jesus Christ, not only for the solemn admission of the party baptized into the visible church, but also to be unto him a sign and seal of the covenant of grace, of his ingrafting into Christ, of regeneration, of remission of sins, and of his giving up unto God through Jesus Christ, to walk in newness of life. . . (Chapter XXVIII)

In every clear NT example, the person baptized made a credible confession of faith in Jesus Christ prior to receiving the sacrament. This has been called the Baptist's argument from silence. But that is an unfair charge. To refrain from a practice on which the Bible is silent is

125

not wrong. But to build a positive practice on supposed but unwritten premises is to build on silence.

Every NT text cited to support infant baptism appears empty apart from a strong predisposition to find such texts and presuppositions to impose upon them.

Amazingly, Matthew 19:13, "Suffer the little children to come unto me, and forbid them not, for of such is the kingdom of heaven," has been used frequently by serious theologians to support infant baptism. We share the opinion of B. B. Warfield who said, "What has this [verse] to do with infant baptism? Certainly, nothing directly."[80] Some point has been made of the related passage in Mark where Jesus is said to bless the children, and note has been taken of his placing his hands upon them. But, again, we find no solemn ceremony in this passage indicating that the children were acknowledged to be in the Covenant of Grace. Prayerful calling of God's blessing upon any child would be most natural apart from such restricted significance.

Acts 2:39 has also been pressed into service to support infant baptism. "For the promise is unto you and to your children . . ." Usually the sentence is not completed. But the Scripture goes on to add, "and to all that are afar off, even as many as the Lord our God shall call." The context has in view specifically spiritual promises, namely remission of sins and filling with the Holy Spirit. These promises cannot be said to attach themselves to the entire crowd before Peter (the "you" of the text), but only to "as many as the Lord our God shall call." They could not be said to belong to "all that are afar off," but only to "as many as the Lord our God shall call." If that phrase qualifies the first and third parties mentioned, it must also qualify "your children." The promises do not belong unto the children of believers apart from effectual calling. Only those children who receive this saving grace of God may be conceived of as being heirs of the spiritual promises.

---

[80] *The Works of Benjamin B. Warfield*, vol. ix; (Baker Book House, Grand Rapids, MI: 1991) p. 398. Warfield goes on to suggest that the text shows that infants indeed were received by Christ as members of His kingdom.

HOUSEHOLD BAPTISMS

Household baptisms are called upon, by paedobaptists, as evidence of infant baptism in the NT. There are four references: Cornelius (Acts 10), Lydia (Acts 16), the Philippian jailor (Acts 16), Stephanas (1 Corinthians 1). None of the references say that infants were in these houses. Finding infant baptism here is built upon the dual assumption that there were infants in the houses and that *household* must have meant every individual in the household without exception. The last of these is a road we Calvinists have been down with the term "world" in Scripture. The first is very untenable. But the two together cannot be held; for we find in the Bible itself, the pattern of these household baptisms. All of Cornelius' house gathered to hear Peter's preaching. The Holy Ghost fell upon all—they all received the extraordinary gifts of the Spirit. Then, all were baptized. Paul first preached to the jailor's household. Then, all were baptized. After the baptism, all rejoiced believing in God. Hearing the Word and believing upon that preaching can scarcely be attributed to infants. No doubt, the same pattern adhered to other cases of household baptisms. In Lydia's case, there is the most doubt that a woman in business would be nursing an infant. The Bible does not tell us she had a husband, let alone children. Infant baptism can be found here only by those most anxious to do so.

First Corinthians 7:14 is another favorite verse of paedobaptists regarding households. There we are told that children are "holy." The text does not have even vague reference to church membership or baptism. It is talking about mixed marriages in which one spouse is a believer and the other is not. The question is whether such a relationship is proper, moral, or holy for those who were converted after marriage to the unbeliever. Paul reasons from the obvious to the doubtful. It is obvious that your children are not bastards. They were born in wedlock. They are holy. Therefore, it ought to be clear to you that your marriage relationship is holy. Do not feel guilty about it or wish to be free from your obligations. If the word "holy" suggests a covenant relationship or cultic purity, making the children proper objects for baptism, then the unbelieving spouse is also a valid candidate for the sacrament. The verb "sanctify" has precisely the same root and signification as the adjective "holy." And it is the holiness of the spouse that the passage belabors.

With such appalling lack of NT evidence for infant baptism, those who support such a practice have rapidly retreated to OT texts and an argument from the unity of the covenants. The practice of baptizing infants of believers is founded on OT Scripture or upon texts of the NT where suitability for baptizing infants is read into them with a predisposition and presupposition drawn from the OT.

I.   HISTORIC COVENANT THEOLOGY AND INFANT BAPTISM

The argument has hung upon a syllogism that goes something like this: There is a unity between the Old and New Covenants. Circumcision in the Old is parallel to baptism in the New. Infants of believers were circumcised in the Old. Therefore, infants of believers should be baptized in the New. Many tell us that this syllogism is so strong that NT silence is a major argument in favor of their position. The New Covenant is so like the Old and baptism so parallel to circumcision, that unless the NT absolutely forbids the baptism of infants, it must be practiced. As B. B. Warfield said,

> It is true that there is no express command to baptize infants in the New Testament, no express record of the baptism of infants, and no passages so stringently implying it that we must infer from them that infants were baptized. If such warrant as this were necessary to justify the usage we would have to leave it in completely justified. But the lack of this express warrant is something far short of forbidding the rite; and if the continuity of the church through all ages can be made good, the warrant for infant baptism is not to be sought in the New Testament, but in the Old Testament when the church was instituted, and nothing short of an actual forbidding of it in the New Testament would warrant our omitting it now.[81]

---

[81] *The Works of Benjamin B. Warfield*, vol. ix; (Baker Book House, Grand Rapids, MI: 1991) pp. 399-400, in an article entitled "The Polemics of Infant Baptism."

OBJECTIONS AND FLAWS

Immediately we Baptists raise our *first* objection. There is here a serious *hermeneutical flaw*. How can a distinctively NT ordinance have its fullest—nay, its only foundation—in OT Scripture? This is contrary to any just sense of Biblical Theology and against all sound rules of interpretation. To quote Patrick Fairbairn:

> There cannot be a surer canon of interpretation, than that everything which affects the constitution and destiny of the New Testament Church has its clearest determination in New Testament Scripture. This canon...strikes at the root of many false conclusions and on the principle which has its grand embodiment in Popery, which would send the world back to the age of comparative darkness and imperfection for the type of its normal and perfected condition.[82]

If you allow OT examples to alter NT principles regarding the church, you have hermeneutically opened the door to Rome's atrocities. It is upon such rules of interpretation that the priest and the mass have been justified. We find the clearest expression, of that which is normative for the New Covenant's ordinances, in the New Covenant revelation.

Secondly, there is a *theological flaw*. It is nothing new for Baptists to adhere to Covenant Theology. They have done so since their inception in the Seventeenth Century. We conceive of God's dealings with man in a covenantal structure. We believe that every covenant made with man since the Fall is unified in its essence. In all ages there has been one rule of life—God's moral law. God's standard of righteousness was the same before Moses received the Ten Commandments, and it is the same today. There has been but one way to salvation in all historic covenants since the Fall. The gospel by which Adam was saved is the same as that by which we are saved. Genesis 3:15 declares a salvation that is wholly of grace through faith in Christ. The basic differences between the covenants of history in these essential matters are those of Biblical Theology. The promises of the gospel have become clearer with each succeeding age of revelation, though the promises have been

---

[82] *The Interpretation of Prophecy*; (Banner of Truth Trust. Edinburg, Scotland: 1964) p. 158; it is also further developed in pp. 245-246.

identically the same. The moral law has been more fully expounded, though never changed. So we agree about the unity of the covenants recorded in the Bible. But paedobaptists have been negligent in defining the diversity in the administrations of the Covenant of Grace. As Dispensationalism has erred when it has failed to see the essential unity of the covenants since the Fall, many serious errors have arisen from a failure to acknowledge diversity in these historic covenants. An example may be seen in the Reformers' failure to distinguish church and state. In the administration under Moses, the church was coextensive with the state. In the administration of Christ, the extent of church and state are not to be thought identical. In the Mosaic economy, magistrates administered the church and prophets made their authority felt in government. In the Christian administration of Grace, a strict sense of the church separate from the state must be maintained. We must define the diversity as well as the unity.

Paedobaptists have unconsciously recognized a difference between the OT and the New with respect to the constitution of the church and subjects of their ordinances. In the Old Covenant, adult sons and servants were circumcised, and thus incorporated into the visible church. Now, only the infants of believers are baptized. In the Old, children came to the Passover at a very young age. Now small children are not admitted to the Lord's Table. Whence this change? When the principle of diversity is formulated, it will exclude infants from the sacrament of baptism. Jeremiah 31:31-34 is pivotal to expressing the diversity of covenant administrations. It is quoted in Hebrews 8 and again in 10 to prove that "Christ is mediator of a better covenant." There is an emphatic contrast made in verses 31 and 32. The differences are so striking and dramatic that one covenant is called "new" and it is implied that the other is old. The Jews under the Old Covenant were warned that revolutionary changes would be made. The covenant in force was inadequate except to prepare for the New. So surpassing is the glory of the New that it should lead them to look for the demolition of the Old. The passage suggests two vital distinctions ushered in by the effusion of the Spirit. This effusion made a change in administration possible.

The *first* difference is found in Jeremiah 31:33. The Old Covenant was characterized by outward formalism. The New would be marked by inward spiritual life. This is not an absolute distinction but it is a marked contrast. Of course, there was spiritual religion and heart commitment to God in the OT. Abraham's faith would put ours to shame. We must wonder if any but Christ Himself ever equaled the prayer life of David addressed in the Psalms. Moses spoke to God as face to face. Yet, these are refreshing streams in the midst of OT attention to outward, formal, national religion. There is a mass of outward rules, a history of formal religion, a ponderous identification of church and nation. Relatively little attention is given to inward life. If a man is circumcised, he is counted a Jew. If he is conformed to outward practices, he is called clean and welcome at the ceremonies of worship. Paul tells us that this system of religion was like the strict tutor who tells a child what to do at every turn.

But the NT church is come of age. It is, by way of contrast, inward, spiritual and personal. Certainly there is outward formality in the New Covenant, but it is minimal; the most formal ceremony calls attention to the inward. The NT presses personal self-examination everywhere and constantly makes spiritual application of its truths. There is a notable shift to questioning experience of grace at every point.

Jeremiah 31:34 suggests the *second* distinction. There will be a marked contrast in the knowledge of those in the New Covenant. As the coming of the Spirit will add a new dimension of life to the church, so He will add a new dimension of light. "From the least to the greatest" in the New Covenant will know the Lord. The subject matter of their knowledge will not be shadows but the living reality of Christ. The mysteries hidden in the Old will be made known to them. The manner of instruction will shift from repetitive ceremonies, for they will all know the Lord. So then, we will expect the New Covenant to stand in contrast with the Old in that its members have greater life and light.

This diversity is nowhere more evident than in the ceremonies of worship. Worship in the NT presents us with a most striking contrast with OT ordinances. This can be illustrated by looking at the Lord's Supper, which finds a counterpart in the OT Passover. The great spiritual truth of redemption by blood is figured in the Passover, but it is somewhat obscured beneath an outward and formal atmosphere. Then, too, the ceremony mixes the figures of personal redemption and national deliverance. Even those who had no acquaintance with spiritual redemption observed it. This they should have done; for their national life arose from the historic event remembered. Very young children came to the Passover as participants that, by it, they might ask the significance and as they grew older, come to understand the redemption figures. (cf. Exodus 12:24-27, etc.)

In the NT, things are quite different. First Corinthians 11:23-30 gives instruction for the most formal ceremony of the New Covenant. Here very young children must not come. Only the "worthy" with "discernment" are welcome at the feast remembering our redemption. It is not marked by any of the nationalism of the Old Covenant. Each person is charged to "examine himself" before daring to partake. He must find himself "worthy" – a personal recipient of grace. He must have "discernment" – that inward, spiritual light that peculiarly marks this covenant. Light and life are prerequisites of joining this most outward and formal act of worship.

The same is true of the waters of baptism. This ceremony does not desert the New Covenant's pattern to revert to the Old. It belongs to those who are "worthy" and have "discernment." Repentance and faith are everywhere demanded as prior conditions for baptism.

Thirdly, there are a number of ***exegetical flaws*** in the paedobaptist theology. Many have reasoned thus: "Infants of believers were circumcised in the Old Covenant. Therefore, infants of believers should be baptized in the New." Though in Abraham's case faith preceded circumcision of his children, this cannot be said to be the rule of the Old Covenant rite. There were times when faith in the subjects of circumcision or in their parents was all but ignored. In the time of Joshua, an entire nation was circumcised in a day. There was no concern for personal election or personal faith. It was clearly administered as a sign of the outward privileges in belonging to the elect nation. Circumcision was never withheld because a parent had no faith. Even when the prophets denounced the Jews for being uncircumcised in heart, they did not suggest that the sons of these unconverted Jews be excluded from the rite of circumcision. To attempt to find a warrant for seeking faith in the fathers of those who are baptized in these OT texts is wholly unsatisfactory.

It is also said that just as baptism is a sign of heirship to the spiritual promises of grace in the New Covenant, circumcision was a sign of heirship to the same spiritual promises in the Old. This is only partially true. Baptism is a sign of spiritual blessing in Christ and only that. Circumcision, too, depicted unity with Christ in His death and heirship to spiritual blessings (cf. Colossians 2:11-13). But there was more to its significance. The distinctive aspects of the covenants cling to their signs just as surely as the common elements of the covenants do. In the Lord's Supper and the Passover, redemption by blood is signified. Yet, they differ in this: The Old ceremony suggested the outward and national aspect of that administration. The New ceremony stresses the inward and personal aspect in its administration. So circumcision could be given to 13-year-old Ishmael, who, Abraham was assured, would not be a partaker of the spiritual blessings. But for him and other non-elect Jews, it was proper by circumcision to be identified with the outward aspects of blessing and administration. It was proper to be circumcised as the literal seed and heir of the literal land and as one by whom, according to the flesh; the Messiah would come, while not being of the spiritual seed and heir of heaven. Baptism has no merely earthly significance. There are no blessings figured in it that can be conceived of apart from an experience of grace.

Much weight has been placed on the formula "Thee and thy seed" in Genesis 17. Paedobaptists insist upon an outward, literal significance of the term "seed." In their scheme, the New Covenant counterpart to Abraham's seed is the physical offspring of believers. This is done while totally ignoring the fact that the NT says a great deal about the covenant with Abraham, for it is central to NT religion. Romans 4, Romans 9, and Galatians 3 and 4, especially Galatians 3:7 belabor the point that believers, and believers alone, are the seed of Abraham. These texts further insist that the promises which are spiritual and eternal belong to no merely physical seed.

In Romans 9, Abraham's immediate, physical offspring are discussed. Some were of the flesh; some of the spirit. There was a personal election within the family election. Abraham could not look upon his own immediate seed as heirs of the promises. "They which are the children of the flesh, these are not the children of God: but the children of the promise are counted for the seed" (v. 8). How can believers today lean upon the promise to Abraham which is clearly interpreted in the NT and find for themselves a greater expectation for their children than Abraham had a right to? The NT is not silent about this seed. It tells us they are believers alone!

Lastly, there are *practical flaws* in the paedobaptist theology. Those who sprinkle infants are on the horns of a dilemma. Either they must tamper with the definition of baptism to make it signify something less than personal spiritual union with Christ as the Bible clearly teaches; or they will be driven to teach infant salvation or presumptive regeneration. If the first course is chosen, one must also corrupt the NT view of the church and its discipline. If some who are less than saved are properly to be considered as members of Christ's body, there is a great deal of stress with the NT's view of membership and fellowship. If the second course is chosen, one's pedagogy will be affected. How are parents and pastors to address the children if they are viewed as joined to Christ? Unfortunately, much paedobaptist literature written for children reflects a tendency to address them as believers, not as in need of evangelism. Note the interesting historic dispute on this subject by paedobaptist theologians J.H.Thornwell and R.L. Dabney on one hand, and Charles Hodge on the other.

SUMMARY

IN THE OLD COVENANT, ALL THAT WAS SPIRITUAL WAS IDENTIFIED WITH AN OUTWARD NATION. IN THE NEW COVENANT, ALL THAT IS OUTWARD IS IDENTIFIED WITH A SPIRITUAL NATION.

II.   HISTORICAL PERSPECTIVE

I can sympathize with students who are wrestling with the problem of baptism. I can remember when I wished to be convinced of the paedobaptist position. There would be many practical advantages. Another forceful factor is the great history of godly men who were paedobaptists, especially the Reformers and Puritans. But as history gave me the problem, so it suggested a solution. Paedobaptism is clearly tied to sacralism in church history. After Constantine and his associates succeeded in getting across the idea that church and state are coextensive, baptism identified a person not only as a member of Christ's church but also as a citizen of the state. The Anabaptists in the Middle Ages were not so concerned about the subjects and mode of baptism as they were about the purity of the church. Believer' baptism has always naturally followed the concept of a believer's church. When Zwingli worked closely with Anabaptists (whom he later helped to condemn to death), he had a rather different view of the church from that which he adopted later. Consequently, he had a believer's baptism view. But when he moved to the concept of a state church, he vigorously defended infant baptism.

So, too, in England. So long as the concept of a state church reigned, there was very little interest in a Baptist position. But as soon as the separatist movement arose, the Baptists emerged naturally from the paedobaptist midst. Just as the sacralist principles were drawn from the OT improperly, so the retreat from national religion to family religion has rested upon OT practices. Once the constitution and discipline of the NT church have been rightly conceived, the hangover of infant baptism must fall way.

These are issues over which we do not wish to lose fellowship with paedobaptist brethren. Yet, they are principles which we will not jettison for the sake of fellowship.

APPENDIX I

WAS THERE A COVENANT OF WORKS?

Justin Taylor

REFORMED THEOLOGIANS HISTORICALLY have held to a "covenant of works" (or covenant of creation) between God and Adam. Many evangelical scholars today deny that such a thing existed. I believe that it does.

This following questions and answers cannot do justice to the relative complexity of the debate, but perhaps it will be helpful for the theologically inclined to see why some of us do believe that the Bible teaches there was such a covenant with Adam.

Was there a covenant between God and Adam?

A fruitful way to answer that is by examining the two most common objections to the presence of a covenant in the garden: (1) The Hebrew word for *covenant* isn't found in Genesis 2-3 (it doesn't show up until Genesis 6:18); (2) Covenants have to have either explicit oaths or ratification ceremonies (like animal ceremonies in Genesis 15:7-21), but this is not found in Genesis 2-3.

The first objection commits the *word-thing* fallacy. Words and things are not the same. The absence of a particular term does not entail the absence of a particular concept. For example, Genesis 3 does not contain any of the standard Hebrew terms for sin or transgression, but the concept is obviously there. Consider also that Psalm 89:3 (cf. vv. 28, 34, 39) refers back to 2 Samuel 7 as a *covenant* involving an *oath*, even though 2 Samuel did not use that terminology. So it is with Hosea 6:7, where Hosea says of his generation that "like Adam they transgressed the covenant." Similarly, Isaiah 24:5 says: "The earth lies defiled under its inhabitants; for they have transgressed the laws, violated the statutes, broken *the everlasting covenant*." Furthermore, William Dumbrell argues that *heqim + berith* in Genesis 6:18 and 9:9ff implies a pre-existing covenant (*Creation and Covenant*, p. 26).

The second objection is *reductionistic*, incorrectly defining the word *covenant*. Explicit oaths and ratification ceremonies are sometimes included in covenants, but not always. The promise of a lasting priesthood to Phineas and his descendants is called a covenant (Numbers 25:12-13). Marriage is called a covenant (Proverbs 2:17; Malachi 2:14). David and Jonathan's arrangement with each other is called a covenant (1 Samuel 18:3; cf. 20:8; 23:18; Psalm 55:20).

What then is a covenant?

Gordon Hugenberger defines *covenant* as "an elective, as opposed to natural, [family-like] relationship of obligation established under divine sanction." He sees five necessary elements of a covenant: (1) two parties, one of who is also the divine witness; (2) historical prologue of past benefactions; (3) stipulations; (4) sanctions; (5) a ratifying oath/oath-sign, which argues that all five are present in Genesis 1-3. A simpler definition, which is complementary to Hugenberger's, is proposed by Ligon Duncan: "A covenant is a binding relationship with blessing and obligations." On either definition, it is clear that God and Adam were in covenant with each other, and the parallels between Christ and Adam in Romans 5 confirm this.

Was there a probationary period?

A probationary period is another way of referring to a time of testing that is not perpetual. Genesis 3 does not use terms like "probation" or "testing"—but again, we must be careful not to commit the word-thing fallacy. It is obvious that Job was tested by God and that Jesus was tested when he was thrust into the wilderness by the Spirit—but no terms of testing are used to describe those situations.

The alternative to denying a probationary period is to believe that Adam would remain in his current state for all eternity, assuming that he did not transgress the command of eating from the forbidden tree of the knowledge of good and evil. But I don't think this makes a great deal of sense.

First of all, it would imply that the fall would remain a perpetual possibility for all eternity. Augustine helpfully distinguished between *posse non pecarre* (able to not sin) and *non posse non peccare* (not able not to sin). Adam had the former (he had the ability to refrain from sin), but he didn't have the latter (the inability to sin). Obviously the latter is a greater form of contentment and enjoyment and security in the presence of God. This is what our glorification will entail: we will be in the presence of God in the new heavens and new earth without the possibility of sin. But it makes no sense to me to imagine that such was an impossibility for Adam.

Secondly, the idea of a perpetual probation does not fit well with Adam's *representative* role. The future of man's relationship with God hung on whether or not Adam obeyed. But if there was never a terminus to the testing, then Adam and his posterity would always be dependent upon Adam's obedience. I think absurdities start to happen if we think along those lines. What if Adam's great-great-great grandson sinned? Would the whole world be plunged into sin? It seems so, but that would deny Adam's representative role.

Finally, Paul's parallelism of Adam and Christ suggests a limited probationary period. Christ's obedience to his Father was tested. He passed, and was "declared to the Son of God in power according to the Spirit of holiness by his resurrection from the dead" (Romans 1:4). If Christ was tested and the duration of the test was for a limited time, this suggests that Adam was tested for a limited time as well.

In short, I can think of no good reason to deny a probationary period for Adam. When the whole of redemptive history is considered, I believe that we must understand Adam as having been in a probationary period.

How long was the probationary period to be?

We have no way of knowing. Because the fall was ordained, the biblical authors have no interest in asking that question. But as I indicated above, I don't think it's possible that it was to be eternal.

Was there a blessing offered for Adam's obedience?

Yes. I believe that glorification, symbolized by the tree of life, would be the result of Adam's obedience. While I don't think that Adam and Eve ate from this tree, I don't think that believing that they *did* eat from it would necessarily compromise belief in the creation covenant.

Why don't you think that Adam and Eve ate of that tree before the Fall?

Because I don't believe there is any textual warrant for that conclusion. And I believe it has theological problems.

Both trees were placed in the middle of the garden (Genesis 2:9). Eating of the tree of the knowledge of good and evil—the probationary tree—entailed eternal banishment away from God. Eating of the tree of life—the sacramental tree—entailed eternal life in God's presence. One tree corresponded to the explicit warning: "Eat and die." The other tree corresponded to the implicit promise: "Eat and live."

Yahweh told Adam and Eve, "You may eat of every tree of the garden, but of the tree of the knowledge of good and evil you shall not eat, for in the day that you eat of it you shall surely die" (Genesis 2:16-17). There's no debate that eating of the tree of the knowledge of good and evil was forbidden and that they did not eat from it prior to the fall. But many scholars assume that therefore they *did* eat from the tree of life. But the text doesn't tell us either way. We have to draw an inference from all of the evidence.

First, the text does not indicate that Adam and Eve knew the name or the meaning of the "tree of life."

Second, I see no reason necessitating that they ate from the tree. Again, the text does not say that they did. I tend to think that the fall happened right away, since we have no reason to think otherwise from the way that the narrative reads, coupled with the fact that Eve was not pregnant (despite perfect fertility and perfect obedience to the command to be fruitful and multiply!). Given all the trees in the garden and the limited amount of time, I see no reason why Adam and Eve would necessarily have had to partake of the tree of life.

Third, we'll have to make a determination about the nature of the tree and what it symbolized. Notice what Yahweh says immediately after the fall: "Behold, the man has become like one of us in knowing good and evil. Now, lest he reach out his hand and take also of the tree of life and eat, and live forever—therefore God sent him out of the garden of Eden" (Genesis 3:22-23). The act of eating from the tree of life meant living forever. This *cannot* refer to the immortality of the soul. That was not at stake, for Adam (and all of his posterity) would live forever anyway (either in heaven or hell). Rather, it refers to living forever in the state that one is in. I believe therefore that after the fall God graciously prevented Adam from eating of this tree so that Adam would not be eternally confirmed in this state of sinfulness. Conversely, eating of the tree pre-fall would have meant a confirmation in the state of sinlessness.

My argument is simple: (1) the tree of life was a sacrament that confirmed one's state; (2) Adam's state of sinless fellowship with God was mutable and thus unconfirmed; (3) therefore he did not partake of the tree of life. Note the word "also" (*gam*) in Genesis 3:22: "Now, lest he reach out his hand and take *also* of the tree of life and eat, and live forever." This suggests that Adam had not yet taken and eaten of the tree of life. With reference to the tree of life, the book of Revelation tells us that it is only for those who "overcome" (Revelation 2:7). Reasoning typologically, we are led to believe that since Adam did not overcome, he did not eat of the tree.

But didn't God grant them permission to eat from all of the trees in the Garden?

Yes he did. But here I would distinguish between God's secret will and his revealed will. God's public declaration of his moral will does not always coincide with the hidden counsels of his will. (For example, his revealed will is "thou shalt not murder," but his decretive will was that Jesus was to be put to death). If my analysis of the role of the tree is on track, then God publicly granted permission for Adam to eat from the tree, but sovereignly saw to it that they did not eat from it.

Was there grace in the covenant with Adam?

Most Reformed writers have assumed that the answer to this is yes— for example, John Owen, Herman Bavinck, Charles Hodge, Robert

141

Lewis Dabney, A. A. Hodge, Geerhardus Vos, James Henley Thornwell, and John Murray all argued for the gracious character of the covenant with Adam.

The question is how we are using the term *grace*. As it is used throughout the Bible, grace often has to do with unmerited divine favor which overcomes sin and is applied to sinners. God the Father does not give grace—in this sense—to the Son, the Holy Spirit, or the angels. He only gives this kind of grace to sinners. So one could argue that because pre-fall Adam was not a sinner, God did not give him grace. That would be a sound and true argument I believe.

On the other hand, God provided for all of Adam's needs and manifested his goodness in Adam's life. Adam obviously did not "deserve" to be created. Since these ideas are also associated with "grace," it may be legitimate to apply the term to the pre-fall covenantal relationship with Adam.

In my view, some in the Reformed camp have become linguistic legalists, wrangling over words rather than sufficiently dialoguing over concepts. To be fair, though, I believe critics often make the same mistake, critiquing before they truly understand the terms and intentions of the covenant theologians.

Due to potential misunderstanding, I think it is generally best to avoid the term "grace" when discussing the pre-fall covenant with Adam. I would rather speak of God's freedom, goodness, and enablement with regard to Adam.

Was Adam to obey in his own strength?

This is one of the unfortunate connotations of the label "covenant of works." Many modern evangelicals understand "works" to be "work righteousness" and hence legalistic striving in one's own strength. But this is neither the teaching of the Bible nor the teaching of Reformed theologians on this issue. For example, Francis Turretin wrote: "Man can bring nothing to it from himself, but depends wholly upon God (as to both the promised good and the enjoined duty, to perform which *God* furnishes him with the power)." Although God created Adam with the power to obey, he "still needed the help of God both to actuate these faculties and powers and to preserve them from change." Therefore, there was no debt (properly so called) from which man could derive a right, but only a debt of fidelity, arising out of the promise by which God demonstrated his infallible and immutable constancy and truth" (*Institutes of Elenctic Theology*, vol. 1, pp. 577-578).

Was Adam to exercise faith?

Yes, in the sense that he was to trust God as his treasure. But, not quite in the sense that Paul calls for faith. Paul does not call upon us just to have a general trust in God to provide for all our needs, but also to have a specific trust in Christ to provide for our greatest need: atonement for our sins. Adam needed to trust God to provide for all his needs (which obviously didn't include the righteousness of another).

If Adam had obeyed, would he have merited the blessing of eternal life?

This is a complicated, nuanced question with much historical discussion behind it. The most important thing to note is that "merit," at least as it is used by careful Reformed theologians, does not imply autonomy or libertarian free will. As I understand it, the main use of the term is to denote *obligation*. God (implicitly) promised Adam eternal life if he obeyed. Therefore, God was covenantally obligated to grant eternal life to Adam if he had obeyed. We know this because God was covenantally obligated to raise Christ from the dead, declaring him the Son of God with power (Romans 1:4). Christ fulfilled the required conditions, and therefore God in his justice gave him his due reward. The same would have been true of Adam. God's sustaining and empowering them does not negate his rewarding them in his justice, for it is still *their obedience* (and not another's) that meets the conditions God required. In my view, the most important thing to avoid is the implication that it was possible for the federal head to fulfill his covenantal conditions through obedience and yet God not provide the promised reward. This concept is more important than the terms employed.

ক০০৬

APPENDIX II

COVENANT THEOLOGY IN BAPTIST LIFE

Ken Fryer

𝒜 STUDY OF EARLY BAPTIST CONFESSIONS clearly and indisputably reveals that Baptists affirmed the tenants of Covenant Theology. In England, seven Baptist churches "which are commonly (though falsely) called Anabaptists" wrote *The London Baptist Confession of 1644*, which was relatively short and dealt more extensively with Christology and ecclesiology, in which is stated the following:

> **III.** That God has decreed in Himself from everlasting touching all things effectually to work and dispose them according to the counsel of His own will to the glory of His name...And touching His creature man, God has in Christ before the foundation of the world, according to the good pleasure of His will, foreordained some men to eternal life through Jesus Christ, to the praise and glory of His grace, leaving the rest in their sin to their just condemnation to the praise of His justice. {The Covenant of Redemption}

As Baptists continued to increase in Great Britain, there was the sense that a more thorough and complete confession of faith was needed for their growing congregations. Unsigned in 1677 and officially signed and adopted in 1689, the Baptists published what is known as *The London Baptist Confession of Faith of 1689*; the father of all Baptist confessions. There is no mistaking what they believed. In Chapter 3, entitled *Of God's Decrees*, covenantal language is professed boldly and unashamedly:

3:3 By the decree of God, for the manifestation of his glory, some men and angels are predestinated, or foreordained to eternal life through Jesus Christ...

3:5 Those of mankind that are predestinated to life, God, before the foundation of the world was laid, according to his eternal and immutable purpose, and the secret counsel and good pleasure of his will, hath chosen in Christ unto everlasting glory, out of his mere free grace and love, without any other thing in the creature as a condition or cause moving him thereunto.

In Chapter 4 entitled *Of Creation*, Timothy George notes that there is the implied understanding of a Covenant of Works:

4:3 Besides the law written in their hearts, they received a command not to eat of the tree of knowledge of good and evil, which whilst they kept, they were happy in their communion with God, and had dominion over the creatures.[83]

However, in Chapter 20 the Covenant of Works is stated clearly:

20:1 The *covenant of works* being broken by sin, and made unprofitable unto life, God was pleased to give forth the promise of Christ, the seed of the woman, as the means of calling the elect, and begetting in them faith and repentance; in this promise of the gospel, as to the substance of it, was revealed, and therein effectual for the conversion and salvation of sinners. (*emphasis added*)

The theme is continued in Chapter 6 entitled *Of The Fall Of Man, Of Sin, And Of The Punishment Thereof*:

6:1 Although God created man upright and perfect, and gave him a righteous law, which had been unto life had he kept it, and threatened death upon the breach thereof, yet he did not long abide in this honour; Satan using the subtlety of the serpent to subdue Eve, then by her seducing Adam, who, without any compulsion, did willfully transgress the law of their creation, and the command given unto them, in eating the forbidden fruit, which God was

---

[83] Timothy and Denise George, eds., *Baptist Confessions, Covenants, and Catechisms* (Broadman and Holman, Nashville, Tennessee: 1996) p. 62.

pleased, according to his wise and holy counsel to permit, having purposed to order it to his own glory.

It may be argued that the covenantal language contained in Chapters 3, 4, and 6 of the *"1689"* is not explicitly stated and is implicit, at best. That argument cannot be made, however, regarding the very clear language of Chapter 7, entitled *Of God's Covenant*:

> **7:1** The distance between God and the creature is so great, that although reasonable creatures do owe obedience to him as their creator, yet they could never have attained the reward of life but by some voluntary condescension on God's part, which he hath been pleased to express by way of covenant.

> **7:2** Moreover, man having brought himself under the curse of the law by his fall, it pleased the Lord to make a covenant of grace, wherein he freely offereth unto sinners life and salvation by Jesus Christ, requiring of them faith in him, that they may be saved; and promising to give unto all those that are ordained unto eternal life, his Holy Spirit, to make them willing and able to believe."

> **7:3** This covenant is revealed in the gospel; first of all to Adam in the promise of salvation by the seed of the woman, and afterwards by farther steps, until the full discovery thereof was completed in the New Testament; and it is founded in that eternal covenant transaction that was between the Father and the Son about the redemption of the elect; and it is alone by the grace of this covenant that all the posterity of fallen Adam that ever were saved did obtain life and blessed immortality, man being now utterly incapable of acceptance with God upon those terms on which Adam stood in his state of innocency.

Without contradiction, flowing throughout the Confession is the stream of Covenant Theology, especially as it is seen in the teachings on saving faith, repentance unto life and salvation, and perseverance of the saints:

> **14:2** By this faith a Christian believeth to be true whatsoever in revealed in the Word for the authority of God Himself, and also apprenhendeth an excellency therein above all other writings and all things in the world, so it bears forth the glory of God in His

attributes, the excellency of Christ in His nature and offices, and the power and fullness of the Holy Spirit in His workings and operations: and so enabled to cast his soul upon the truth thus believed; and also acteth differently upon that which each particular passage thereof containeth; yielding obedience to the commands, trembling at the threatenings, and embracing the promises of God for this life and that which is to come; but the principle acts of saving faith have immediate relation to Christ, accepting, receiving, and resting upon Him alone for justification, sanctification, and eternal life by virtue of the *covenant of grace*.

15:2 Whereas there is none that doth good and sinneth not, and the best of men may, through the power and deceitfulness of their corruption dwelling in them, with the prevalency of temptation, fall into great sins and provocations; God hath, in the *covenant of grace*, mercifully provided that believers so sinning and falling be renewed through repentance unto salvation.

17:2 The perseverance of the saints depends not upon their own free will, but upon the immutability of the decree of election, flowing from the free and unchangeable love of God the Father, upon the efficacy of the merit and intercession of Jesus Christ and union with Him, the oath of God, the abiding of the Holy Spirit, and the seed of God within them, and the nature of the *covenant of grace*, from all which ariseth also the certainty and infallibility thereof. (*emphasis added*)

Coming across the Atlantic, to the confessions of faith of the First Baptist Church of Newport, Rhode Island which is arguably the oldest Baptist congregation in America (founded in 1644), Pastor John Clarke wrote an implied acceptance of Covenant Theology:

The decree of God is that whereby God hath from eternity set down with himself whatsoever shall come to pass in time (Ephesians 1:2). All things with their causes, effects circumstances and manner of being, are decreed by God (Acts, 2:23). Him being delivered by the determinate counsel and foreknowledge of God (Acts, 4:28). This decree is most wise: (Romans 11:33); most just: (Romans 9:13, 14); eternal: (Ephesians 1:4, 5; (II Thessalonians 2:13); necessary: (Psalm 33:2, Proverbs 19:21); unchangeable: (Hebrews 6:17); most free: (Romans 9:13); and the cause of all good: (James 1:17); but not of any sin: (I John 1:5). The special decree of God concerning angels and men is called predestination (Romans 8:30). Of the former, viz., angels, little is spoken of in the Holy Scripture; of the latter more is revealed, not unprofitable to be known. It may be defined, the wise, free, just, eternal and unchangeable sentence or decree of God, determining to create and govern man for his special glory, viz., the praise of his glorious mercy and justice; (Romans 9:17), grace and mercy, choosing some men to faith, holiness and eternal life, for the praise of his glorious mercy (I Thessalonians 1:4, II Thessalonians 2:13, Romans 8:29, 30). The cause which moved the Lord to elect them, who are chosen, was none other but his mere good will and pleasure... (Luke 12:32). [84]

Herein is an implied expression of a Covenant of Redemption. Clarke further implied a belief in a Covenant of Grace:

The end is the manifestation of the riches of his grace and mercy, (Romans 9:23, Ephesians 1:6). The sending of Christ, faith, holiness, and eternal life, are the effects of his love, by which he manifesteth the infinite riches of his grace. In the same order God doth execute this decree in time, he did decree it in his eternal counsel (I Thessalonians 5:9; II Thessalonians 2:13).[85]

Additionally, Clarke intimated an affirmation of the Covenant of Works when he wrote, "Sin is the effect of man's free will, and condemnation is an effect of justice inflicted upon man for sin and disobedience..."[86]

Obadiah Holmes, who succeeded Clarke as pastor of the Newport congregation, was exceedingly more explicit than Clarke in his affirmation of Covenant Theology. Holmes wrote in his thirty-five Articles of Faith:[87]

---

[84] Isaac Backus, *A History of New England with Particular Reference to the Denomination of Christians Called Baptists*, vol. I (Boston, MA: Edward Draper), p. 206.
[85] Backus, p. 206.
[86] Ibid., p. 206.
[87] Ibid., pp. 206-209.

Article 3. I believe that as God made the world, so by his word made he man in his own image without sin, and gave him a most excellent place and being, giving him commandment what he should do, and what he should forbear; but through the malice of Satan working with his wife was deceived; for she did eat, and gave her husband and he did eat, which was the first cause of the curse to him, and reached to all his posterity, by which came death natural, and death eternal.

Article 4. I believe in this interim of time the Lord manifested his great love in that word, 'The seed of the woman shall break the head of the serpent,' but enmity was between the two seeds.

Article 6. I believe after that God in his own time chose a people to himself, and gave them his laws and statutes in a special manner, though he had always his chosen ones in every generation.

Article 7. I believe with this people he made a choice covenant to be their God, and they to be his people; which covenant they brake though he was a Father to them, and was grieved for them, and yet did not only give them his laws, but sent his prophets early and late, but they would not hear; and in fullness of time sent his only Son; but as they had abused his prophets, so they killed his only Son.

Article 8. I believe God in his Son made a new covenant, a sure and everlasting covenant, not like that he made with Israel, of which Moses, that faithful servant, was mediator, but a covenant of grace and peace through his only Son, that whosoever believed in him should not perish, but have everlasting life.

Article 9. I believe that all those that are in this covenant of grace, shall never fall away nor perish, but shall have life in the Prince of Life, the Lord Jesus Christ.

It is evident, even to the casual reader, that one of the oldest Baptist congregations in America expressed an affirmation of biblical Covenant Theology.

Not only did the oldest Baptist church in America affirm Covenant Theology, but so did the oldest Baptist Association in America, the Philadelphia Baptist Association, formed in 1707. Elias Keach, taking from his father Benjamin Keach, revised *LBC* to form the *Philadelphia Confession of Faith of 1742*. Keach added two chapters, one on singing of hymns and the other regarding laying on of hands. This confession clearly confirms the Philadelphia Baptist Association's acceptance of Covenant Theology and was adopted by the association in 1742.[88]

The covenantal view of the Philadelphia Baptists soon spread southward as "the Philadelphia Association sent numerous missionaries and church planters throughout the South during the middle and latter eighteenth century. It was responsible for the rapid growth of "Regular Baptist" (which is what Calvinistic Baptists came to be called) churches and associations in the South."[89]

The first Baptist association in the Southern United States was the Charleston Association, formed in 1751. Being greatly influence by the Philadelphia Baptists, the Charleston Association was Reformed in its theology, and in 1767 adopted *LBC*. Having adopted this historic confessional document, the Charleston Association was on record as having embraced Covenant Theology.

The Charleston Association, specifically the First Baptist Church of Charleston, South Carolina, made an invaluable contribution to Baptist life. Not only did the church embrace a Calvinistic theology, but held to Covenant Theology as evidence by their confessional position. First Baptist Church—Charleston was fervent in spreading the gospel and planting churches. It also produced some of the finest theologians and leaders in the United States. Men such as Oliver Hart, Richard Furman, Basil Manly Sr., and William T. Brantley, Sr. "adhered to a confessional Calvinism that made its way through the generations to James Petigru Boyce and formed the foundation of his lifework."[90]

James Petigru Boyce is an example of a Southern Baptist theologian and statesman *par excellence*. Boyce served as Professor of Theology

---

[88] Carol C. Holcomb, "Baptist Confessions of Faith," *Baptist History and Heritage Society;* Available from http://www.baptisthistory.org/contissues/holcomb.htm

[89] Thomas K. Ascol, "From the Protestant Reformation to the Southern Baptist Convention: What Hath Geneva to Do With Nashville?" *The Founders Journal* (Fall, 2007).

[90] Thomas J. Nettles, *James Petigru Boyce: A Southern Baptist Statesman* (Phillipsburg, New Jersey: Presbyterian and Reformed Publishing), 23.

at Furman University from 1855-1859, founded The Southern Baptist Theological Seminary and served as its President from 1859-1888, and served as the President of The Southern Baptist Convention from 1872-1879 and 1888.

Perhaps Boyce's greatest contribution to theology is his *"Abstract of Systematic Theology,"* written in 1887. This volume consistently and forthrightly expresses Boyce's affirmation of Covenant Theology. Consider Chapter XXII entitled *The Fall of Man*, Article III: *This, A Fall Under the Covenant of Works*, which is seen in this extensive quote:[91]

> The fall of Man occurred when he was on probation under the Covenant of works.
>
> Theologians are accustomed to speak of two especial covenants, the one of works, the other of grace. These do not embrace all the covenants between God and man, which indeed have been very numerous. The others most prominently mentioned in the Scriptures are that with Noah, Gen. 9:11-17; with Abraham, Gen. 17:2-14; (repeated to Isaac, Gen. 26:2-5; and to Jacob, Gen. 28:13-15;) with Israel in giving the law, Ex. 24:7; Deut. 5:2, 3; with Moses and Israel, Ex. 34: 27; with David, 2 Sam. 7: 1~16; with Solomon, 2 Chron. 7: 1~22; and that of Nehemiah and the Israelites with God, Neh. 9: 38 to 10: 39. The two covenants of works and grace are spoken of in Gal. 4: 2~31, and are called 'the two covenants' in verse 24. That of grace is the covenant of redemption made by God with his elect, or more properly with Christ, the second Adam, as their representative. That of works is the covenant of the law entered into between God and all mankind through the first Adam, their natural head and appropriate and appointed representative.
>
> A covenant is an agreement between two or more parties by which any one or more things are to be done under the sanction of rewards and penalties. This is the ideal form of a covenant. Some parts of it may he wanting, and still it may be a covenant. Thus there may be penalties and no reward, or reward and no penalties.

---

[91] James P. Boyce, *Abstract of Systematic Theology* (Cape Coral, Florida: Founder Press), pp. 234-237.

Also, the agreement may arise, not from mutual consultation, but from a command given and accepted. This may take place at the time it is given, and with the person to whom it is spoken, or the command may be given, or promise made, to be accepted and acted upon by any who may at any time choose. Thus, between a government and its responsible subjects, law becomes a covenant. Rewards also are promised, as for the killing of dangerous or destructive animals, or for the capture of criminals; or threats are uttered, for violation of the rights of others, either as to life, liberty, or property.

These preliminary statements may remove the difficulties sometimes felt as to the existence of a covenant of works. Law prescribed by God as lawgiver is admitted to exist together with its sanctions and penalties; and, as in human law, so here, no excuse can he made of want of formal agreement; because of the natural obligation to obey.

These facts are, however, more fully applicable to the covenant of works, regarded as the general law of obtaining and maintaining spiritual life, given to all mankind, and still held forth to them, than to the transactions under that covenant connected with Adam's fall. In this latter the elements of a *covenant* more distinctly appear.

I. There are here the two parties to a covenant, God and man; the one prescribing what was to be done, or left undone; the other receiving the command to do or not to do it.
If it be objected to the parties, that God enjoined an act through his sovereign and supreme power and dominion, to which man dared not object; the sufficient reply is that God was no more sovereign lord than man was willing subject. The holy constitution of his nature, rendered his ready acceptance absolutely certain.

II. Here also we find the subject matter of a covenant, the forbidding under penalty the eating of a certain fruit. That which made this properly a part of the covenant, was that man knew that he was commanded not to eat; that he recognized God's right to command, and his duty to obey; that he had a natural inclination towards obedience; and that, accepting the command of God, lie proceeded to submit himself to it. Both the knowledge and assent of man, however, may be absent from the general covenant of works, where it appears under the especial form of law, or duty, whenever that absence is the result of man's sinfulness, and man still be held responsible. But in an innocent being this knowledge and assent are essential to responsibility. Yet that very innocence, because of the holiness of the creature's nature, secures such assent to God's law when known as completes the more formal covenant.

III. The third element of the covenant is the penalty, death, the meaning of which will be hereafter examined. The threat of God "thou shalt surely die" (Gen. 2:17), was known not only to Adam, but to the woman also, as appears from her conversation with the serpent. Gen. 3:1-3.

IV. The promises made or implied constitute a fourth element. It is questioned whether promises were added to the covenant. None appear in the narrative. None were necessary to make this a covenant. None are necessarily involved except such as are implied as attendant upon the result of obedience. These, therefore, may be first stated as being thus implied, and such considerations may be added as, from our further information, suggest that others were actually expressed. Those implied are:

(1) Continuance of God's favour, which having been bestowed on them as innocent creatures, would continue to be shown if they should not disobey his commands.
(2) Continuance of their happy, holy condition until by their own act they should forfeit it.
(3) Continuance, therefore, unless in like manner forfeited, of the immortality natural to their souls; and as to their bodies, continuance of their then existent condition, or, if any change should occur, a change into higher forms, bestowed for their greater happiness.
(4) To this may be added that their children, so long as this state of innocence should continue, would be born with like innocent and holy natures.
These results of obedience are implied.
(1.) In the benevolent holiness and justice of God's nature. Even if never stated to Adam as promises, they would be naturally inferred by him from his knowledge of God.
(2.) They are also implied in the very threat against disobedience, if, as we shall hereafter see, that threat involved not merely natural

death, but also, and chiefly, that absence of God's favour and communion which is the death of the soul.

If death would follow disobedience, then life ought to follow obedience—life in all the opposites to death, and therefore life both of the body and the soul.

It would seem, therefore, that there ought to be no question that these blessings were believed by Adam to have been made dependent upon his obedience to God's commands.

But not only were these thus implied, but the fact that life was promised 'is clearly taught in other passages of Scripture. Lev. 18:5; Neh. 9:29; Matt. 19:16, 17; Gal. 3:12; Rom. 10:5'. [Hodge's *Outlines*, p. 311.]

Another prominent Charlestonian,[92] Basil Manly, Jr., made significant contributions to Baptist life. Timothy George writes, "When Southern Seminary opened its doors in Greenville, South Carolina in October, 1859, Manly was one of the four founding faculty members. His official title was Professor of Biblical Introduction and Old Testament although he fulfilled many other roles as well in his long association with this institution. One of his first assignments had been to draft a confessional statement, the *Abstract of Principles* (as it was called) for the new school.

Boyce, in setting forth the plan for the Seminary, had stressed the importance of a solid theological foundation. Drawing upon earlier Baptist confessional standards such as the First (1644) and Second (1689) London Confessions, Manly proposed an *Abstract of Principles* which consisted of twenty articles of faith ranging from the Scriptures to the Last Judgment. These articles of faith were included in the Fundamental Laws of the Seminary. Every professor was expected to teach in accordance with and not contrary to these articles. Failure to do so would be considered grounds for his resignation or removal by the trustees."[93]

---

[92] Basil Manly, Sr. served as pastor of First Baptist Church of Charleston, South Carolina from 1826-1837. Manly, Jr. moved to Tuscaloosa, Alabama with his family at the age of twelve when Manly, Sr. became President of the University of Alabama.

[93] Timothy George, "Basil Manly and the Bible Doctrine of Inspiration," *The Founders Journal* (Spring, 1993)

There are other examples of expressions of Covenant Theology in Baptist life. A circular letter by the Georgia Baptist Association, under the direction of moderator Jesse Mercer, written in **1828** with the inscription, "Scriptures that Support our Constitution" bears consideration. Notice the explicit affirmation of Covenant Theology:

> **4th**. We believe in the everlasting love of God for his people and the eternal election of a definite number of the human race to grace and glory; and that there was a *covenant of grace or redemption*, made between the Father and the Son, before the world began, in which their salvation is secure, and that they in particular are redeemed.[94]
>
> Further, this article derives proof, Zechariah 9:11, As for thee also, by the blood of thy covenant, I have sent forth thy prisoners out of the pit wherein is no water. And again, Hebrews 8:6, He is the *mediator of a better covenant*, which was established upon better promises; and 9:15, And for this cause, he is the mediator of the New Testament, or covenant, (*diatheke* is, the word used in both cases,) that by means of death, for the redemption of the transgressions that were under the first Testament, that they which are called might receive the promise of eternal inheritance.[95]
>
> And Hebrews 13:20, and part of 21, Now the God of peace that brought again from the dead our Lord Jesus, that great Shepherd of the Sheep, through the *blood of the everlasting Covenant*, make you perfect in every good work. Psalm 2:8; 110:1; and Hebrews 8:9, 10, *establish the Covenant between the Father and the Son*.[96]
>
> Such as were chosen, and for whom the Covenant was entered into, were redeemed by Jesus Christ, as appears from Ephesians 1:7, in whom we have redemption through his blood, the forgiveness of sins according to the riches of his grace.[97]

---

[94] The Georgia Baptist Association, "Circular Letter: Scriptures that Support our Constitution," Baptist Home Page; Available from
http://baptisthistoryhomepage.com/1828.cl.ga.committee.html
[95] Ibid.
[96] Ibid.
[97] Ibid.

Licking Association of Baptists (Kentucky) is another example of Covenant Theology in Baptist life. In a Circular Letter written in **1811** by Ambrose Dudley, it is confessed, "It is truth, that we are poor sinners, and as such, deserve to be thrown from the presence of God, and certainly will be, if not found in the Covenant of Grace, and our names written in the Lamb's Book of Life."[98]

A Declaration of Faith by the first Baptist church in Ohio, Columbia Baptist Church of Cincinnati, confessed in **1790**:

> **3rd** We believe before the world began God did elect a certain number of souls unto everlasting salvation whom He did predestinate to the adoption of children by Jesus Christ from his own free grace and according to the good pleasure of his will and that in of this gracious design he did make a Covenant of Grace and peace with his Son Jesus Christ, on the behalf of the elect persons.[99]

In **1806**, the Mississippi Baptist Association declared in its Articles of Faith:

> **6.** We believe all those who were chosen in Christ before the foundation of the world are, in time, effectually called regenerated, converted, and sanctified; and are kept by the power of God, through faith, unto salvation.[100]
>
> **7.** We believe there is one mediator between God and man, the man Jesus Christ, who by the satisfaction which he made to law and justice, 'in becoming an offering for sin' hath, by his most precious blood, redeemed the elect from under the curse of the law, that they might be holy and without blame before him in love.[101]

---

[98] Licking Association Of Baptists (KY) "Circular Letter, 1811 By Ambrose Dudley," Baptist Home Page; Available from
http://baptisthistoryhomepage.com/1811.ky.licking.dudley.html
[99] Columbia Baptist Church, Cincinnati, Ohio, "Declaration of Faith," Baptist Home Page; http://baptisthistoryhomepage.com/columbia-hist.html
[100] Mississippi Baptist Association 1806, "Articles of Faith," The Reformed Reader; Available from http://www.reformedreader.org/ccc/1806msbc.htm
[101] Ibid.

The first Baptist church in Louisiana (Half Moon Bluff) was short lived. A few months after the first church was formed, a small group of Baptists on Big Creek (Louisiana) asked the Mississippi Baptist Association for help in the organization of a church. Soon afterward in **1813**, the Mount Nebo Baptist Church was organized and is the second oldest living Baptist church in the state. Shortly after organizing, articles of faith were adopted.[102]   In these articles of faith a belief in Covenant Theology is unmistakably articulated:

> **3rd** We believe that before the world began, God did elect a certain number of Men unto everlasting salvation whom he did predestinate to the adoption of children by Jesus Christ of his own free Grace and according to the good pleasure of his will; and that in pursuance of his Gracious design he did contrive and make a Covenant of Grace and peace with his Son Jesus Christ on the behalf of these persons wherein a Saviour was appointed...[103]

> **5th** We believe the Lord Jesus Christ being set up from everlasting as the Mediator of the New Covenant and he having engaged to be the surety of his people...[104]

From the Baptists in England to the first Baptists in America, from New England southward to South Carolina and Georgia, westward to Kentucky and Louisiana, to significant Baptist leaders and theologians, it has been demonstrated that Baptists, from their inception have affirmed and expressed a belief in Covenant Theology. This is but a rough sketch. The serious reader and student can do further research and discover that in this appendix; only the "hem of the garment" has been touched regarding the subject of Covenant Theology in Baptist life. Search and then ask yourself the question of why there was a major theological paradigm shift in Baptist life in the 1920s, especially among Southern Baptists. Then retrace the steps of your Baptist forefathers and embrace the truths that made them strong and caused them to do exploits.

かe~ら

---

[102] Glen Lee Greene *House Upon a Rock: About Southern Baptists in Louisiana* (Alexandria, Louisiana: Louisiana Baptist Executive Board: 1973), 62
[103] Greene, p. 63.
[104] Ibid., p. 63.

APPENDIX III

How is the New Covenant not like that which has come before?

Kenneth Puls

God's Covenant in the Old Testament

The Old Testament included external elements necessary because Christ was coming in the flesh. The outward elements served God's purpose to prepare for the promise of a Seed and to foreshadow what Christ would accomplish in redemption. With the advent of Christ in the New Testament these external elements pass away.

The Old Covenant involved the preservation of a physical seed, a physical nation, from which the Seed would come.

In the Old Testament God's Covenant extended outward to encompass a physical people. Not all who were included in the outward covenant possessed the spiritual realities of the covenant. Only a spiritual remnant was true Israel. For they are not all Israel who are of Israel (Romans 9:6). One could be born under the outward covenant, receive the outward seal of the covenant and not be part of the true Israel.

Because Old Testament Israel encompassed both a physical and a spiritual nation, the Law was written down upon tablets of stone. (Only spiritual Israel had the Law of God upon their hearts.) Those who had only the letter of the law in stone, and not the Spirit, were condemned and killed by the law. Apart from the promise of grace, the Law can only bring bondage, condemnation, and death.

The worship of God in the Old Testament focused upon ceremony and ritual in the Temple in Jerusalem, which foreshadowed and taught of a future work that Christ, the Messiah, would come and accomplish in history.

In the Old Testament God physically manifested His presence in one place: in the pillar of cloud, in the pillar of fire, on the mountain, at the mercy seat in the tabernacle or temple. The physical nation of Israel had limited access to His presence, hindered by physical barriers.

In the Old Testament the knowledge of God comes through the teaching of the priests and Levites. God's Word is revealed though His prophets. The knowledge of God is limited and incomplete. Only spiritual Israel was taught by God's Spirit in their hearts.

The seal of the Old Covenant was outward: Circumcision of the flesh (Genesis 17:10-14).In the Old Testament saints were members of a physical kingdom with the promise of a physical inheritance and possession of land. They were children in bondage under the elements of the world until the fullness of time when Christ would come (Galatians 4:3-5) and the outward elements of the covenant would be fully removed.

All the external elements in the Old Testament (including the physical land and temple) foreshadowed the better spiritual realities of the New Testament.

In the Old Testament the saints were served by a king, by prophets, and by priests who were themselves sinners and in need of God's forgiveness and grace. They offered sacrifices year after year which could not take away sin.

God's Covenant in the New Testament

In the New Testament Christ has come. He is the substance. All the types and shadows of the Old Testament pointed toward Him. Now that He is come, the externals of God's Covenant in the Old are obsolete, growing old, and ready to vanish away (Hebrews 8:13).

The New Covenant provides for the preservation of a spiritual seed, a holy nation, the body of Christ.

In the New Testament the outward elements of the covenant are fully removed. All who are in the covenant know the Lord and are the true Israel. For they shall all know Me (Jeremiah 31:34). One cannot be physically born into the New Covenant. It is not of blood (John 1:13); one must be born again. The bond of flesh no longer places children in the covenant. (Jeremiah 31:29).

Under the New Covenant the Law of God is written upon the hearts and minds of all who are in the Covenant. All of God's people in the New Covenant have the Spirit of God, Who alone gives life. He does not write the Law in stone, where it can only bring bondage, condemnation, and death, but upon the heart. For those who possess the promise of grace, the Law is not burdensome, but a delight (Romans 7:22).

In the New Testament God is seeking those who worship Him in spirit and in truth from the heart. We celebrate the reality of Christ's work accomplished and completed in history.

In the New Testament the Spirit of God is present in the hearts of all God's people (not just a remnant). His temple is the heart of every member of the community of faith (2 Corinthians 6:16). We now have unlimited and bold access to His throne of grace (Hebrews 10:19-25).

In the New Testament the knowledge of God comes through the ministry of God's Spirit in the hearts of all His people. No more shall every man teach his neighbor (Jeremiah 31:34). The knowledge of God is full and complete, revealed in Christ. God has spoken by His Son (Hebrews 1:2), through the Scriptures.

The seal of the New Covenant is inward: Circumcision of the heart (Romans 2:29; Philippians 3:3).

In the New Testament saints are members of a spiritual kingdom. The kingdom of God is within you (Luke 17:21). We no longer seek a physical inheritance in the land or a political theocracy (Hebrews 11:13-16; 13:14). The kingdom of God is not of this world (John 18:36). On this earth we are strangers and pilgrims (1 Peter 2:11). Our citizenship is in heaven (Philippians 3:20). We desire a better, heavenly country (Hebrews 11:16).

In the New Testament Christ is our Prophet, High Priest, and King. He offered a perfect sacrifice once for all time that removed the sin of His people completely. (Hebrews 7-10). We are now all members of a royal priesthood who continually offer a sacrifice of praise. (Hebrews 13:15; 1 Peter 2:9).

THE ASSOCIATION OF REFORMED BAPTIST CHURCHES OF AMERICA

The Association of Reformed Baptist Churches of America was founded on March 11, 1997. On that day the first General Assembly met to establish a charter membership of 24 churches from 14 states. Since then we have grown to more than 70 churches and continue to expand by the providence of God. We invite you to inquire further for more information and how your church can become a member of this national association.

Our association is recent, but our churches have been established many years in their communities and share a rich heritage that extends back to the Reformation. We encourage you to browse the various parts of our web site posted below and learn more about us!

Jesus prayed in John 17 for His disciples to be brought to complete unity so that the world would know that the Father sent Him. ARBCA is designed to advance Christ's kingdom by providing a fellowship in which churches of common confession may find mutual encouragement, assistance, edification, and counsel, and participate in cooperative efforts such as home and foreign missions, ministerial training, and publications, along with other such endeavors deemed appropriate by the Association.

There are many large cities and towns without a Reformed Baptist church. A number of churches are desirous of planting churches in these desperately needy areas. What one church cannot do, many working together can. ARBCA can assist local churches with their church planting efforts. ARBCA can also help churches seeking pastors and pastors seeking churches.

Reformed Baptists have a distinct theology and practice. Because of this, the Association plans to develop its publishing house to meet the printing needs for Christ-centered, church-centered, and covenantally Baptistic literature. Look to the opposite page to see some of the material that is presently available from our publishing arm, Reformed Baptist Publications.

ARBCA
PO BOX 289
Carlisle, PA 17013
(717) 249-7473
www.arbca.com

Other Titles by Solid Ground

Grace and Glory: *Sermons from the Chapel of Princeton Seminary* by Geerhardus Vos is a wonderful series of God-centered sermons.

Notes on Galatians by J. Gresham Machen is a reprint that is long overdue, especially in light of the present-day battle of the doctrine articulated in Galatians.

The Origin of Paul's Religion by J. Gresham Machen penetrates to the heart of the matter and speaks to many of the contemporary attacks upon the purity of the Gospel of Christ.

Biblical and Theological Studies by the professors of Princeton Seminary in 1912, at the centenary celebration of the Seminary. Articles are by men like Allis, Vos, Warfield, Machen, Wilson and others.

Theology on Fire: Vols. 1 & 2 by Joseph A. Alexander is the two volumes of sermons by this brilliant scholar from Princeton Seminary.

A Shepherd's Heart by James W. Alexander is a volume of outstanding expository sermons from the pastoral ministry of one of the leading preachers of the 19th century.

Evangelical Truth by Archibald Alexander is a volume of practical sermons intended to be used for Family Worship.

The Lord of Glory by Benjamin B. Warfield is one of the best treatments of the doctrine of the Deity of Christ ever written. Warfield is simply masterful.

The Power of God unto Salvation by Benjamin B. Warfield is the first book of sermons ever published of this master-theologian. Several of these are found nowhere else.

Mourning a Beloved Shepherd by Charles Hodge and John Hall is a little volume containing the funeral addresses for James W. Alexander. Very informative and challenging.

Call us at **1-205-443-0311**
Send us an e-mail at **mike.sgcb@gmail.com**
Visit us on line at **www.solid-ground-books.com**

CPSIA information can be obtained
at www.ICGtesting.com
Printed in the USA
FFOW03n1424310118
44796484-44937FF